SKETCHES
OF
SOCIAL LIFE IN INDIA

SKETCHES
OF
SOCIAL LIFE IN INDIA.

BY

C. T. BUCKLAND

GYAN

Published by

Gyan Publishing House
5, Ansari Road
Daryaganj, New Delhi-110002
Phone: 011-47034999, 9811692060
E-mail: books@gyanbooks.com

Distribution Network
gyanbooks.com
India, USA, Canada, UK, Australia

ISBN: 978-93-6280-187-6 (PB)
First Published, 1884

2nd Impression 2024

Printed at: Gyan Press, Delhi.

SKETCHES OF SOCIAL LIFE IN INDIA
Author: C. T. BUCKLAND

SKETCHES OF SOCIAL LIFE IN INDIA.

SKETCHES

OF

SOCIAL LIFE IN INDIA.

BY

C. T. BUCKLAND, F.Z.S.

FATHER OF THE BENGAL CIVIL SERVICE IN 1881.

LONDON:
W. H. ALLEN & CO., 13 WATERLOO PLACE,
PALL MALL. S.W.

1884.

PREFACE.

The first two chapters of this book were published more than a year ago in the *Army and Navy Magazine*, and are reprinted with the kind permission of the proprietors, Messrs. W. H. Allen & Co. The other chapters were written about the same time, as articles for the same Magazine, but not being sufficiently within the scope of a military and naval periodical, it was resolved to produce them in the present form. The author, in the course of a long career in the Bengal Civil Service, has held nearly all the appointments which he has attempted to describe in connection with that service, and he had many opportunities of becoming acquainted with all the mechanism of Indian government, as seen from Calcutta and the Lower Provinces of Bengal. In his attempt to give a sketch of social life in India, it must be remembered that he is writing chiefly of the Lower Provinces of Bengal. He has endeavoured to avoid anything which might give personal offence, and he would gladly adopt as his motto, "*Ridentem dicere verum quid vetat?*" It is hoped that this book may afford some entertainment to those who have been in India, and that it may be of use and interest to those young men who are thinking of devoting themselves to a professional career in India. It only remains to observe that these papers were written before the recent agitation in connection with the Ilbert Bill, but it has not been found necessary to alter anything that had been written as regards either the English residents or the native community.

20, Ashburn Place,
7th February, 1884.

CONTENTS.

SKETCHES OF SOCIAL LIFE IN INDIA.

CHAPTER I.

THE VICEROY AND HIS COURT.

THERE are two different classes of people who know very little about India. First there is your old Indian, who fancies that he knows all about the presidency, say Bombay, in which he spent his time, but is as ignorant of the presidencies of Bengal and Madras as he is of China and Japan. Secondly, there is your real rural Englishman, who has had no relations or connections in India, and is, perhaps, still grieving over the untimely fate of some old friend who went out and suddenly died in India. There undoubtedly still exists in many English circles a considerable amount of ignorance and a deep-rooted prejudice against all things Indian. It is possible that this prejudice may be traced back to the ways and manners of the East Indian Nabobs of the last century, whose pompous display of wealth, suspected to have been acquired by dubious practices, was an offence and a scandal to the quiet English country gentleman, and, indeed, to all who did not contrive slyly to make a profit out of the Nabob's money. The Nabob himself was usually shy and awkward, and almost always irritable and irascible, and remarkable for his peculiar social manners; so that it came to pass, that a general idea prevailed that the picture presented by the Nabob in England was but a reflection and reproduction of the social manners which he had acquired during his sojourn in the distant East. How far this feeling was correct it is not our present purpose to inquire. The race of Nabobs has come to an end. The pagoda-tree of fabulous memory no longer bears its golden fruit. An enormous change has come over the habits and manners of those Englishmen who now practically colonise India. For though colonisation is usually spoken of in a different sense, the British inhabitants of India are virtually a colony. The individual colonists may change, but as fast as one man goes another steps into his place; and thus it comes to pass that over the whole length and breadth of India there is now a large and continually growing colony of English families, who endeavour to maintain their old home feelings and to keep all those old surroundings which remind them of the land of their birth, to which they all hope in due course to return. They treasure in their hearts a warm and kindly remembrance of their old home, and they live in the fond belief that they may be well and kindly thought of by those whom they have left behind.

It is, however, certain that much ignorance, not unmixed with the old anti-Nabob prejudice, still prevails regarding the ways and habits of our countrymen in India. The most absurd inquiries are addressed to people who have been in India, which doubtless sometimes provoke answers more suited to the intellectual acquirements of the questioner than in actual accordance with the real facts of the case. If your fair and charming companion at a dinner-party persists in her conversation in filling all Indian houses with snakes and scorpions, she will be much more gratified to hear a few anecdotes which accord with her own assertions, than she would be to learn that it is possible to live for years in some parts of India without seeing either a snake or a scorpion. When recent editions of popular Indian hand-books solemnly inform the reader that rhinoceros hunting is an ordinary amusement in the suburbs of Calcutta, it is much easier to acquiesce in that information than to urge respectfully that alligators may sometimes be found in the ornamental waters of Battersea Park.

One of the greatest changes that has come over India in the last thirty years is to be found in the very great addition that has taken place to the numbers of the non-official classes. Fifty years ago Indian society consisted chiefly of the military and civil servants of the Indian Government. In Calcutta the judges, barristers, and other legal officials formed almost a separate set in the local society. Then came the great merchants, the representatives of the few but famous old commercial houses, whose names were from time to time mixed up with fabulous wealth and hopeless insolvency. In the interior of the country there were many parts where the face of a non-official European was unknown, whilst in some districts a few hardy Englishmen and Scotchmen were to be found engaged in the precarious cultivation of indigo or the manufacture of sugar, or in managing and farming the lands of native land-owners. But, taken all together, the non-official classes of Englishmen were counted by hundreds, where now they are numbered by thousands. In such a community the Governor-General and the members of his Council were pre-eminently the makers and rulers of society; and as in those days these great official people did not all run away to the hills of Simla and other mountain stations as soon as the weather became hot, the impress of their authority was never wanting in social life. The great annual ball at Government House in Calcutta on the Queen's birthday (which is usually one of the hottest days of the year) was looked forward to by all classes with the deepest interest and anxiety, and it was on this occasion especially that the pretty half-caste girls of Calcutta had an opportunity of making their *début* in the grand world, to make havoc of the hearts of the gay young civilians and cadets and ensigns who were then amongst the acknowledged rulers of the society in the capital.

But those were the days before the mutinies, and before the introduction of railways. The steamers of the Peninsula and Oriental and other companies had not then a monopoly of passengers, and people still went out to India in sailing vessels round the Cape of Good Hope. There are some warm-hearted politicians who imagine that the change of Government in India, by the substitution of the name of the Queen for that of the old East India Company, has conferred inestimable benefits on all people who dwell in India. In one sense they are quite correct, because the benefits referable directly to this cause are almost as inestimable as they are invisible to the mind's eye. But that a great change has come over the land since 1857 is undeniable. The well-known Mr. John Marshman, the historian of India, used to say that it was impossible to do any good in a country like Bengal, or for a people like the Bengalis, because, according to their national proverb, it was "impossible to carve rotten wood." But the introduction of railways has almost falsified the national proverb. Wherever the iron road pervades the country, it gives a new basis of strength and vitality on which a new growth of life can arise. It is no exaggeration to say that this new power has affected materially the whole European and native community, and has worked and is working the most important social changes. By the use of the railway, the Viceroy and the provincial governors are enabled to resort without anxiety to the cool hill stations, from which the electric telegraph flashes their orders to the labourers in the hot vineyards of the plains. By the railway the wealthy and pious Hindoo pilgrims are enabled to proceed in ease and comfort to remote sacred shrines, and at such a moderate cost that their money-bags still contain ample store to propitiate the priests in charge of the temples and their idols. The wandering Caubul merchant no longer commits himself and his caravan of camels to a tedious march of several months to reach Calcutta, but stows himself, with his Persian cats and rugs and pomegranates and other wares, in the third-class carriage of a railway, and finds himself at his journey's end in a few days, instead of months. Within the last few years it happened that a distinguished political officer was summoned from Quetta to Calcutta, a journey of about two thousand miles by railway, to be consulted by the Viceroy. He had scarcely returned to Quetta when a telegram came summoning him back to Calcutta for a further consultation. So that in less than a fortnight he twice traversed the whole continent of India without any great fatigue, and with very little risk to his health.

It would, perhaps, be difficult to find a stronger contrast in illustration of the increased facilities of travelling which railways in India afford, than is to be found in Bishop Heber's celebrated journal, written about 1824, and in Mr. James Caird's letters describing his recent visit to India in 1879. They both covered nearly the same ground, though their routes lay in different directions. The Bishop started eastwards by boat from Calcutta to Dacca. He took six weeks on his journey, and his chaplain died of illness contracted on the way. By railway and steamer Mr. Caird travelled from Calcutta to Dacca in about twenty-four hours. The Bishop set out again in his boat from Dacca to Allahabad, and accomplished the distance, which is about seven hundred miles, in nearly three months. Mr. Caird was enabled to cover the same distance by railway and steamer in three days. The Bishop went forth on horseback from Allahabad with a military escort to protect his tents and baggage, and made an erratic journey through the then independent province of Oude, and to the hill-station of Almora, and eventually through the principal cities of Rajpootana and Western India until he reached Bombay. This pilgrimage necessarily lasted for several months, as his progress was at the rate of about ten miles a day. Mr. Caird, by the help of the railways, started from Bombay and reached Allahabad, after visiting Oude, in about ten days. In fact a fortnight, or at the longest a month, is now deemed amply sufficient time for the travelling tourist to do India. And what is the result? In Bishop Heber's journal the reader will find a series of faithful and kindly observations on the ways and manners of the people amongst whom he lived and journeyed day after day, whilst his remarks on the state of the crops are sound and intelligent, as being based on his own practical knowledge of the cultivation of the glebe of his English parish. In the letters of Mr. Caird and in other modern travellers, we find too many hasty conclusions such as are usually formed from rapid and imperfect observation. Mr. Caird's knowledge of English agriculture may be unrivalled, but he had about the same opportunity of forming an opinion on Indian agriculture and the various measures necessary for its development, as the hero of the old story in "Scholasticus," who was expected to form an opinion of a house from the inspection of a single brick.

With the improved facilities of communication with England, and also between the various parts of India, a great change has necessarily come over the social habits of Englishmen residing in India. The official classes have lost a great portion of their social influence, whilst the non-official classes have gained a corresponding advantage and position. This is due to many causes, partly to the mere force of numbers, partly to the different distribution of wealth and means, and in some places individual character has, as usual, contributed considerably to the change. We will endeavour to go into some detail as to the difference which is shown in different stages and classes of society, and it will be for our readers to judge whether the profit or loss, the gain or the disadvantage, lies with the present or the past generation.

The Governor-General of India has always been the chief fountain of honour, and the first pillar of the state and of all social influence. His dignity is now still further enhanced, as, under the title of Viceroy, His Excellency shines forth as the direct representative of his sovereign. But as regards this high position, so much depends on personal character and manners, that it would be difficult to arrive at a decision when contrasting the quiet dignity of Lord Canning or the genial presence of Lord Mayo with the haughty extravagance of Lord Ellenborough or the solid and imperturbable majesty of Lord Dalhousie. There is, however, a more persistent and successful endeavour under the modern *régime* to maintain the credit of Government House for hospitality, and what is vulgarly called entertainment. There are now ten people to be entertained where there was formerly only one. The Viceroy lives for eight months of the year at Simla, and for the remaining four months in Calcutta. At Simla the society is, to a great extent, official, swollen by the numerous representatives of the army with their families, who seek refuge at Simla from the fearful heat of the plains of Northern and Central India. A weekly dinner at Government House, and two or three State balls, suffice at Simla to provide for the gratification of the visitors, whilst the staff and household of the Viceroy, especially with Lord W. Beresford to guide them, used to contribute not a little to keep the ball of amusement rolling in all phases of society.

When the Viceroy and his suite descend to Calcutta in November, the usual notices are issued for a levee and a drawing-room. On several occasions in recent years an attempt has been made to induce all the ladies of Calcutta to appear at the drawing-room with trains and feathers, but it has usually been left optional to them, the result being that the trains and feathers which do appear sometimes afford a sort of clue to the character and social position of the lady who wears them. The ladies who have the private *entrée* at Government House make their bow first before the Viceroy's wife, and then, with the gentlemen of their families, stand on either side of the Viceroy's throne, in a sort of sacred semi-circle, in support of the Queen's representative. The ladies who have not the private *entrée* are then admitted, and presented in the order of their arrival. There are always a few beautiful and graceful English women in Calcutta, who would be an ornament to any European Court. Very few native ladies appear at the drawing-room, but a stout and stately olive-complexioned East Indian (half-caste) lady sometimes sweeps by, waving her ostrich plumes and with a train of golden tissue twenty-four feet long; and she is, perhaps, succeeded by a lady from Burmah, where the lower part of the female costume scarcely amounts to a single petticoat. When the drawing-room is over, the ladies who have been presented are ushered into the upper drawing-room or ball-room of Government House, where they can rejoin the gentlemen under whose escort they came in their carriages to Government House. Long buffets are laid out with everything that is needed to refresh them after their exertions, and the band plays for about an hour, until they quietly disperse to their homes. This is an excellent arrangement, as it affords the ladies a suitable opportunity of displaying their dresses, and seeing their friends' dresses, and receiving the admiration to which they are entitled. About four hundred ladies usually appear at the drawing-rooms in Calcutta.

The levee for men, which is held a day or two before or after the drawing-room, is a much less interesting, but more fatiguing business. Every man in Calcutta, European or Native, who can get the necessary vouchers for his admission, seems to make it his duty and his pleasure to attend. If he attends the levee, there is the chance that he may receive an invitation to dinner at Government House, or, more probably, to one of the great balls or "at homes" which are annually given by the Viceroy. Therefore, every European assistant and every clerk in the merchants' offices, and banks, or in Government employment, strives for admission to the levee. Every native gentleman, who can obtain letters commendatory, is anxious to make his obeisance before the Viceroy. The great people, such as the members of Council, the judges of the High Court, the members of the Board of Revenue, and the secretaries of the Government, with the several military chiefs and heads of departments, who have the private *entrée* to Government House, are first presented to the Viceroy, and pay the penalty for their precedence by having to stand during the whole levee on either side of the Viceregal throne. A distant noise like the roaring of the sea is next heard, and there presently appears a heated and excited party of the representatives of the outside public, who have been successful in struggling to the front places and in being admitted first through the series of barriers by which the impatient crowd, numbering about twelve hundred, has to be restrained. The struggle to get to the front is something fearful until the protection of the first barrier is reached. Coat-tails are torn off, swords in their scabbards broken, hats treated as foot-balls, as the body of eager aspirants crushes forward. It is almost a comfort to find a soft place on this occasion between two fat and portly native gentlemen, who suffer grievously, but still gladly, for the honour and glory which they presently hope to attain. Several of the early barriers which have been already mentioned are kept against the crowd by non-commissioned officers, but as the candidates approach the throne, they come under the manipulation of the A.D.C.s and other officers on the staff, whose brilliant appearance sometimes seems almost to fascinate the mind of the uninitiated. At last the foremost comer is bidden by the A.D.C. to advance, card in hand, to meet his Viceregal master. He steps forward and hands his card to the Military Secretary, who announces his name in a loud voice, and the next two paces bring him in front of the Viceroy. Some men make a proper obeisance and pass on. Some give a little sort of a nod to the Viceroy, and, looking bewildered, try to retire by the way they had advanced, when an A.D.C. promptly interferes. A difficult case sometimes arises, when the Viceroy, on recognising someone to whom he desires to be gracious, puts forth his hand to be shaken. This proceeding being observed by the man who comes next, he cheerfully puts forth his hand to be shaken by the Viceroy, but meeting with no reciprocity, he slinks off in dismay.

Military uniform and the ordinary evening dress of civilians are the principal costumes. But the native gentlemen who appear present every variety of dress, more or less national or fanciful, according to their taste. A great deal of misunderstanding exists, unfortunately, on the subject of native dress. It is the present fashion with educated natives to despise the old simple national costume, and to profess to regard it as typical of servile submission to a conquering race. A young educated Bengali would not condescend to wear a robe of fine white muslin and a white turban (containing, perhaps, a hundred yards of the finest muslin), in which dress his father and grandfather were so becomingly arrayed. A new kind of turban has been invented for them of some coloured stiff material, and their body-dress is a long sort of single-breasted Noah's Ark garment, of cloth or silk, reaching nearly down to the ancles. White stockings and patent leather shoes or boots are considered very correct, and sometimes cloth trousers are visible above the boots, but not unfrequently this portion of European costume is wanting, and the native garment called a *dhooti* lurks oeneath the Noah's Ark coat. Thus arrayed, the wealthy young Bengali presents himself before the Viceroy. A comparatively recent fashion for educated native gentlemen is to appear in their college caps and gowns, which indicate the high degrees that they have taken in the local universities. But, perhaps, really the proudest man among them is he who assumes a regular English evening costume, with his head bare like a Briton, his beautiful black hair richly oiled and curled, and a white tie round his neck, and white kid gloves on his hands. From this it is evident to all the world that his mind and body have really achieved practical independence, and that he is on perfect equality with his foreign rulers.

But the levee must come to an end. The officers of the Volunteer corps who have been engaged on duty are presented to the Viceroy, and, finally, the native officers of the native regiments which have been on duty are brought up and go through the very graceful ceremony of proffering the hilts of their swords to His Excellency. The hundreds who have attended the levee then disperse to their homes, no refreshment being provided after the levee, although, as has been mentioned, the ladies, after the drawing-room, are more kindly treated. Every man, therefore, seeks the earliest opportunity of quenching his thirst at his own house or club, and the pipe of peace probably consoles him for all the loss of temper and damage of apparel which he sustained in struggling into the presence of the Viceroy. It is only fair to admit that it is reported in the Indian papers that at Lord Ripon's levees a successful attempt has been made to prevent all the crushing and struggling among the men for priority, which had been so disgracefully prevalent at previous levees.

It has been mentioned above that most of the men who go to the levee, do so in the hope of getting an invitation to dinner at Government House, or, at least, to one of the balls, or "at homes," or garden-parties, which are given by the Viceroy in the course of the season. With regard to the dinner invitations, there are always one or more experienced A.D.C.'s on the Staff who are careful to weed the dinner-list judiciously; but with huge weekly or bi-weekly dinners of sixty or eighty persons, the Viceroy generally manages to gratify the vanity, and satisfy the appetite of most of his ambitious visitors and their wives in the course of the season. Doubtless much heart-burning exists on the part of those who are not invited to these feasts, especially when they know that any friends of their own immediate circle are invited, and find themselves omitted. The A.D.C.-in-waiting sometimes has to receive an irascible visitor who wants to know the reason why he and his spouse have not been invited to dinner; and letters of remonstrance on this subject are believed to be by no means uncommon. But "a mild answer turneth away wrath," and there is no instance on record of the A.D.C. having ever suffered from the much-threatened horsewhip.

There are very few native gentlemen who care to meet their European brethren at the dinner-table, and they, therefore, seldom appear at the Government House dinner-parties. It is not that our native friends, especially of the wealthy and educated classes, do not appreciate a dinner in the English or European style, but, for reasons which it is not easy to explain satisfactorily, they seem to prefer to indulge themselves with such meals in the privacy of their own houses. It has also been considered advisable, of late years, not to invite native gentlemen to the balls at Government House. The reason for this can be put in a very simple form. The native gentleman does not bring his wife or daughters to the dance, and he himself does not dance. Therefore his presence in a ball-room is unnecessary. This explanation does not cover the whole of the case, but it is sufficient for our present purpose. Almost everyone knows that native ideas on the subject of dancing differ almost entirely from our own. Perhaps it may be permissible to mention one very notable exception to ordinary native habits in the matter of dancing. We refer to a young Rajah, the ruler of a semi-independent province, who has had the good fortune to be brought up under most judicious and capable English tutors and guardians. This young prince is equally good at polo and rackets and lawn-tennis, and most other European sports. He is a first-rate shot and a very fair horseman. In a ball-room his success is unmistakeable, and as he has the manners of an English gentleman (than which we can offer no higher compliment), he is also fortunate in having so mastered all the difficulties of waltzing, that it is generally understood that he is accepted by the best dancers in a ball-room as a very welcome partner. He wears a sort of semi-military costume, with a velvet tunic slightly braided with gold, and it would be difficult to find any man more thoroughly conversant with all social etiquette, or more familiar with the colloquial niceties of the English language.

In order, therefore, to suit the tastes of the great majority of the native gentlemen who wish to display their loyalty, the Viceroy gives several evening parties, which are known as "at homes"; and these are varied by garden-parties in the gardens adjoining Government House, which take place about sunset, and are continued until dark, when the grounds and adjacent buildings are lit up with a brilliant illumination. The "at homes" take place indoors, and as there is no dancing or music they are not very lively entertainments; but an "at home" everywhere depends chiefly on the capacity of those who are invited to entertain themselves from their own resources, and this element is not strong amongst our native friends. At a garden-party they are much more at ease and happy. They can bring their little grand-children to the garden-party and see the pleasure which the children enjoy, and the admiration which they sometimes attract. This is rather a curious feature in native society. The grandfather cannot bring out his wife or his daughter, according to native usage, so he appears in charge of his grand-children. The grandfather himself may be of the mature age of forty-five. His married daughter is perhaps about twenty-five, and the grand-children are usually under ten years of age. Little native girls of that age are exceedingly picturesque, and often absolutely pretty, but about that age they are married, and withdrawn from the gaze of the outer world. Certainly the customs and habits of our native friends are mysterious; but there is no occasion to pity them because they firmly believe that though their ways are not as our ways, they are in every respect much preferable and superior to those of the European strangers.

We may say one word, before parting, regarding the balls given by the Viceroy at Government

House in Calcutta. There are occasionally what are called small dances, when about 150 or 200 of the "upper ten" are invited; but a real *dignity-ball* means the issue of above 1,200 invitations, which are intended to include all whose names are on what is called "the Government House List." It is a very pretty and interesting sight when the room is crowded, about 10 o'clock, and the Viceroy with his wife and their private friends, and staff, make their appearance in procession and take their places for the opening quadrille. A sacred space is corded off for the Viceroy's quadrille, the ends of the cords being held or guarded by some of the handsome young privates of the Viceroy's native body-guard, in their gorgeous scarlet uniforms and plumed head-dresses. These body-guard men are quite a study, as they stand gazing imperturbably on the dazzling scene. In the early and crowded part of a Government House ball, it is usually expedient to walk about with someone who is able to criticise the appearance and dresses of the ladies. There are representatives of nearly all nations, and some of the Armenian and Jewish ladies are conspicuous for the splendid diamonds and gorgeous semi-oriental dresses which they wear. The ball-room usually looks very bright with the numerous military uniforms and political and diplomatic costumes, which present a happy contrast to the ordinary civilian evening dress. It might be deemed impertinent to go into detail regarding the dresses of the ladies, but a critical eye can usually distinguish the fashions of at least three years, the latest arrived belles exhibiting the modes of the latest London season, whilst many are about a year out of date, and a few still adhere to the dresses which were in vogue two years before. However, the dancing is always carried on with much spirit, and there is no lack of good partners for those pretty girls who are seen to dance well. About 12 o'clock supper is announced, and a move is made to the supper-room on the next floor, where there is never any want of all that is needed to cheer the heart of man or woman. Usually the Viceroy retires soon after supper, and probably has an hour of telegrams and urgent business to get through before he can go to sleep. The rest of the company carry on the ball until the programme is exhausted, and even the most large-hearted *chaperones* are obliged to ask the A.D.C.'s to allow no more extra dances. And so, about 3 o'clock in the morning, Government House relapses into silence and repose.

CHAPTER II.

MEMBERS OF COUNCIL AND LIEUT.-GOVERNORS OF BENGAL.

In the Indian hierarchy H.E. the Commander-in-Chief of India comes next in rank and position to H.E. the Viceroy and Governor-General. But although to all military men "the Chief" is naturally the most important personage professionally, it is seldom that "the Chief" and his *entourage* make a very deep impression on the social life of the country. There is a sort of military court-circle whilst the Chief resides at his summer quarters at Simla, where he holds periodical levees, and gives dinner-parties and picnics, and sometimes a ball, but that is chiefly to his official friends and acquaintances. When the Chief descends to Calcutta, he occupies the house assigned to him in Fort William, and thereby unintentionally assumes a sort of exclusive position against non-official society. It is not every merchant or barrister or other civilian who has time or courage to face all the sentries, and cross all the drawbridges of the fort, which hedge the divinity of the Chief. The fort is a sort of large and ingenious rat-trap, in which there is one cardinal rule—that you must not retrace your steps, or go out by the gate through which you entered. Sentries bristle at every corner, sometimes English, sometimes native soldiers; all evidently full of aversion to stray visitors. So that when you have at last scaled the Chief's staircase and written your name in his visiting-book, under the supervision of a good-looking A.D.C., you make your retreat with considerable satisfaction, and with a feeling of profound relief as soon as you find yourself again outside the precincts of the fort. The official position of the Chief is also somewhat anomalous, as he is a member of the Viceroy's Council, although there is also a Military member of the Council, whose function it is to advise the Viceroy on military matters, and thus apparently to keep the Chief under a sort of control. Theoretically it may be presumed that the Chief should be at the head of his army, wherever it is engaged in war. This was actually the case when Lord Gough was Commander-in-Chief in the great campaigns in the Punjab, when the Sikh army threatened our existence. And still more so was it the rule during the mutinies of 1857–58, when Lord Clyde, as Commander-in-Chief, shared all the perils and labours of those brave men who then reconquered India. But in later times, and also before the mutinies, it was not always so. It is a matter of tradition that Sir William Gomm was the best man at Simla at the interesting game of cup and ball, there being only one civilian who could, but would not, beat him at it. In the days of Sir William Mansfield his excessive zeal in the domestic economy of his household led to scandals and a court-martial, which has become only too famous in military history. When Lord Napier of Magdala was Chief, the state of India was generally peaceful; and although the late genial Commander-in-Chief would gladly have taken the command in person in the late Afghan campaign, it was not permitted to him to do so. It is to be hoped that no opportunity may be afforded to the present Commander-in-Chief, Sir Donald Stewart, to take the field in person; but, if the occasion should arise, there are few who know Sir Donald Stewart who would not again gladly serve under him.

We come next to the Members of the Viceroy's Executive Council. The word "executive" indicates a marked distinction from the "additional" members of the Council of the Viceroy. "Executive" means £8,000 a year. "Additional" means no pay, or merely a slight increase of an existing official salary. There are seven members of the Executive Council. The Commander-in-Chief and the Military member have been already mentioned. There is the Legislative member, who is usually an English barrister. Two members of the Civil Service represent, by turns, one the interests of the Bengal or the North-Western Provinces, the other the rival Presidencies of Bombay or Madras. There is also a member in special charge of Public Works; this appointment was abolished, but has been restored. Finally, there is the Financial member, who may be either an ex-M.P., like Mr. Wilson or Mr. Massey, or an ex-civilian, like Sir Charles Trevelyan and Sir Richard Temple, or an ex-artilleryman, as in the case of Major Baring. Each of these fortunate men has a salary of £8,000 a year. The pay used to be £10,000, but hard times brought about a reduction; and one of the first victims of the reduction announced his intention of meeting it by reducing his charitable and other subscriptions by 20 per cent. It is hardly necessary to say that people in the position of a Member of Council are considerably victimised for subscriptions of every sort, from contributions to statues in honour of departing Viceroys down to the most useful and practical charitable institutions. Thirty or forty years ago the Member of Council was a man of much mark and social influence in Calcutta. The Governor-General, in those days, might go touring through remote provinces; but the Members of his Council remained permanently in the capital, and carried on the ordinary business of government. The princely entertainments of Sir Charles Metcalfe as a Member of Council are not even yet forgotten. It is almost distressing to those who remember Mr. Dorin's hospitable establishment, to see the fine old house now let as a lodging-house, with half-a-dozen different families occupying flats or rooms in it. Mr. Dorin had the credit of never having been beyond sixteen miles from Calcutta, and then only on a visit to the Governor-General at his country seat at Barrackpore. But it would be tedious and invidious to mention more of the old and honoured names. Now matters are very different. The whole Council migrates annually to Simla with the Viceroy, and several of the members look upon their winter residence in Calcutta with almost equal apprehension for their health and their purse. As they contrive to live about eight months of the year at Simla, they naturally make it their head-quarters and home. Some of them still keep up a house in Calcutta, which they let during their absence at Simla. But those who have no house of their own have either to pay an enormous rent for a furnished house for the Calcutta season, or live at a boarding-house or at one of the clubs. The chief evidence of their presence in Calcutta consists in the swarm of scarlet-coated servants who hang about their doors. As they cannot keep carriages at Simla, where only the Viceroy uses a carriage, they have to hire their equipages from the job-masters in Calcutta, for which they have, of course, to pay *season prices*. Almost all the time that they spend in Calcutta they are groaning over the expenditure which they have to incur, for a Member of Council has arrived at that time of life when the acquisition of money is more pleasing than the spending of it. As they stand on their dignity, and do not condescend to call on any new comers, they are able to contract the circle of their acquaintances; and thus they avoid the expense of giving many large dinner-parties. Some are, by their nature, more hospitably and socially disposed than others, and less intent on economy. But the Member of Council is no' longer a very important element in the Indian social system, and his absence from the social circle would, perhaps, be not much more noticed than his absence from the Council Chamber would be regretted by some ardent reformers who have no sufficient respect for his official position.

Perhaps it may be convenient to explain briefly the official relation which exists between the Viceroy of India and the Members of his Council. All the orders of the Government of India issue in the name of the Viceroy, and the language of the official letters is so couched, that the uninstructed public believe that each subject has received the personal consideration of the Viceroy. But in reality, the work that comes before the Government of India is divided into several departments—the Political, Financial, Home, Legislative, Military, and so on. The Viceroy usually takes direct cognisance of only one department, viz. the Political; a separate Member of Council has the immediate control of each of the other departments. The official papers are submitted to the Viceroy and to each member of the Council in boxes, after they have been duly cooked and noted on by the departmental secretary and his underlings. In all ordinary matters of business, the member in charge of the department passes his own orders, which is usually done by signing his initials in approval of the secretary's proposals, and these orders issue in the Viceroy's name. In any difficult or doubtful cases, the member directs that the papers are to be circulated to the Viceroy and his colleagues, and under this division of labour the work of the country is easily carried on. Subjects on which there is any considerable difference of opinion, or of very great importance, are reserved for oral discussion by the Viceroy and his colleagues at their weekly or special meetings in the Council Chamber. As the Viceroy is held to be personally responsible to Parliament for the administration of India, his opinions usually prevail in Council, and those Councillors who are wise in their generation concur with their lord and master, whilst there remains to the unconvinced and independent Councillor the privilege of recording his dissent, for his own satisfaction, and sometimes in the pleasing hope that his minute may be laid before Parliament and read by a sympathising British public. Notwithstanding all this, there are some who have entertained a doubt whether the use of each member of the Council is altogether equivalent to the amount of his salary, and have accordingly dared to recommend the abolition of some of these appointments. But such persons are obviously little better than heretics and infidels.

If we have not put a very high estimate on the social value of the Member of the Council during his sojourn in Calcutta, let us try to depict him as he dwells in his distant mountain home at Simla. Here he lives a sort of suburban life, sometimes physically, sometimes metaphorically, in the clouds. Doubtless there are some glorious days and even weeks of fine weather at Simla, and the change of climate to the hills at first seems delicious to those who have come up from a long and hot journey by the railway, or who have been detained by their duty in the plains until the hot winds and all the horrors of the hot season have begun. But if Simla has its advantages, it also has its serious drawbacks. There is seldom a visitor who has not promptly to summon the aid of the doctor, and only last year the chemists' shops were almost cleared out of all their stores of chlorodyne. The highly rarefied air at an elevation of 7,000 feet above the level of the sea affects the circulation and breathing of almost all new comers, and those who have any organic affection are likely to suffer very seriously, unless they are exceedingly prudent. It is not, therefore, quite a perfect paradise. And there are many days when the clouds seem to come down upon the mountains, and the thick mists roll up from the valleys to meet the clouds, and you cannot see your next neighbour's house, or even the trees of your own garden. Then, too, the rain decends furiously, and rattles upon the wooden or corrugated iron roofs of the houses with a deafening noise. A flash of lightning dazzles your eyes, and the sharp crack like a pistol-shot tells you how near to you it passed, followed by an awful crash of thunder, which echoes and rechoes from every neighbouring mountain and valley. In such a scene as this, you may perceive, if a lucid interval permits it, the Member of Council riding home from a meeting at the Viceroy's residence, looking like a bathing-machine man, and caparisoned from head to foot in drenched waterproof garments. Riding, however, is an exercise not always congenial to the age of a Member of Council; and in this case he has to be carried in a sort of sedan-chair, locally known as a *jhompon*, with which four or more hill-men toil along, groaning and grunting and perspiring, partly from the weight of their burthen, and partly from the heat of the coarse but bright-coloured clothes which they wear as their master's livery. There is a sort of grim satisfaction in seeing the sleek Member of Council exposed to some discomfort from the weather, as he *must* go to his Council meeting, whatever the state of the weather may be. This, however, fortunately for him, happens only about once a week. On other days he is master of the situation, and can sit over his fireside, with his office-boxes round him, regardless of the elements. If the weather is fine, he will walk out on the Mall, with his pony or *jhompon* in attendance, and escorted by one or more of his scarlet-coated satellites. He may loiter about his garden, or he may look on at a lawn-tennis party, or he may go so far as to have a party for lawn-tennis at his own house. But even at Simla the Member of Council is not much given to hospitality. It was said of a certain legislative member, who shall be nameless (and it is now an old tale), that the smoke was never seen to come out of his kitchen-chimney after his own frugal mid-day meal had been prepared. There is, perhaps, something to be said on behalf of the Legislative Member, as he is usually an elderly barrister of great but previously unappreciated ability, who is sent out to India by some political friend to make what money and reputation he can in the five years for which his appointment lasts. There have been brilliant exceptions to this rule within the last half-century, but we need not dwell upon these details. We regret to have to come to the conclusion, speaking broadly, that the Member of Council, whether it be at Simla or Calcutta, is too frequently a social failure, and, as has been already imperfectly suggested, sometimes almost an official nonentity, or at the best a sort of political paradox.

It might perhaps have been more correct, according to the official table of precedence, to have given priority of mention to the Governors and Lieutenant-Governors of Provinces. But for the present we will consider that the Governors of Madras and Bombay are, after their kind, though less in degree, analogous in their own kingdoms to the Viceroy. The Lieutenant-Governors of provinces, on the other hand, stand out with a stronger sense of personality, and in the case of the Lieutenant-Governor of Bengal the position becomes more accentuated, partly from the vast importance of the charge, and partly from the more immediate contact in which the Lieutenant-Governor is placed as regards the Viceroy when the latter is in residence in Calcutta.

It may be new to some people to be told that in Calcutta there are at times no less than five "Lord Sahebs," as the natives call them. There is the great Lord Saheb, *i.e.* H.E. the Viceroy. There is the little Lord Saheb, *i.e.* the Lieutenant-Governor of Bengal. There is the Lord Saheb of Calcutta—at least, that was the title in use when Sir Stuart Hogg was Lord Mayor of Calcutta. There are also the Military Lord Saheb or Commander-in-Chief, and the Lord Padre Saheb, *i.e.* the Bishop. But of all these several lords it turns out that the little lord, *i.e.* the Lieutenant-Governor of Bengal, is of most importance, at least for social purposes, in the eyes of the Calcutta community. The Lieutenant-Governor of Bengal, since the creation of the appointment in 1853–54, has always been a distinguished member of the local Civil Service, with two notable exceptions—when the political and personal connections of Sir George Campbell and Sir Richard Temple caused them to be foisted on a province with which they had little or no previous official connection.

The Lieutenant-Governor of Bengal rules over a kingdom containing so many thousands of square miles, and so many millions of people, that no person of reasonable intellectual capacity ever tries to recollect the actual figures. His dominions are not quite so extensive as the British realms, on which it is said that the sun never sets; but the sun gets up a long time earlier in the eastern portion of the Bengal province than it does in the western portion of it, so huge is the extent of the territory. As to the millions of people, it is more easy to talk or write of them than to form a correct conception of them. You may understand that there are probably a million of mites round a well-kept cheese. But there are nearly fifty districts, or cheeses, each with its million of mites, under the care and custody of the Lieutenant-Governor of Bengal, and even this estimate inadequately represents the full number of his subjects. And yet, if it can be believed, there is not one of these many million mites who is not able and authorised to represent to the Lieutenant-Governor of Bengal any personal grievance or injustice from which this individual mite believes himself to be suffering. And, as a fact, not a day passes on which considerable numbers of these mites do not address the Lieutenant-Governor directly by letter, representing their personal wants and grievances. In a large number of their cases an inquiry is made by the Lieutenant-Governor to ascertain if the grievance is real, and if it has not already received due attention from the proper authorities; or the complainant is put in communication with the local officers who are competent to deal in the first instance with the subject of his grievance.

The Lieutenant-Governor of Bengal does not, however, always repose upon a bed of roses, and the head that wears a crown usually finds some thorns in it. However, let us consider the good side as well as the less favourable side of the case. The Lieutenant-Governor has a salary of £10,000 a year to begin with, and he has also the privilege of making a monthly contingent bill, as it is called, in which certain items vaguely called sumptuary expenses are charged upon the public revenues. He has a private secretary and one or more A.D.C.'s at his disposal, and occasionally a special physician to look after his health. He is provided with two official residences—one called "Belvedere," in the neighbourhood of Calcutta, and the other called "The Shrubbery," in the mountain station of Darjeling. He has a splendid yacht or state barge at his disposal, in which he can traverse the rivers that intersect his dominions, where railways and ordinary roads do not provide the means of communication. He has his special trains and state carriages on the railways. He has an escort of irregular cavalry whenever he takes his walks, or rides, or his carriage-drives, abroad; and his gates are guarded by sentries,

3

both native soldiers and policemen. His scarlet-coated satellites are only less numerous than those which may be seen on the Viceroy's establishment. In short, though he is called the little lord, in contrast with the great lord or Viceroy, he is so much alike in all his surroundings that Pompey is very like Cæsar, and Cæsar is very like Pompey, but particularly Pompey.

The Lieutenant-Governor of Bengal may be said to be the permanent head of the social system in Calcutta. It is to him that the native community especially look as the fountain of honour, and as the dispenser of patronage in his province. Nor are the European portion of the public by any means backward in seeking His Honour's favour and patronage on behalf of themselves and their young friends and relations who are sent out to India to find a livelihood. It is a fact that there is hardly a member of Her Majesty's Government or of Her Majesty's Opposition who has not an application lying before the Lieutenant-Governor for an appointment to be given to some connection or acquaintance. If such applications come all the way from England, it may be imagined how much more numerous they must be from those persons who live in India, and have more or less a personal acquaintance with the Lieutenant-Governor's existence. For every appointment that he bestows he has the satisfaction of knowing that the old proverb is true, and that whilst the successful candidate is probably ungrateful, there are at least nine other disappointed men who henceforth look upon the Lieutenant-Governor as an enemy. It must not be supposed that the Lieutenant-Governor is unprotected against the swarm of applicants for places and patronage. He has his official secretaries and his private secretaries to guard the outworks, and with good reason "*difficiles aditus primos habet.*" The inexperienced applicant may be baffled in many ways. He may be informed that he has not applied through the proper channel. He has knocked at the private door when he ought to have gone to the official gateway. If he succeeds in effecting an entrance, and in obtaining an interview with the private secretary, he is met with courteous words, but he must be very fortunate or very strongly backed up if he is permitted to get a glimpse of the Lieutenant-Governor. He is requested to leave his papers and his address, and to await an answer. The young man departs, feeling confident that he has effected a lodgment, and that he has created a favourable impression, and so he goes away with a light heart. He little knows that as soon as his back is turned, the private secretary, in an unimpassioned and business-like manner, passes on the papers to a clerk, with an order, "Give this gentleman our No. 1 form." There are three or four stereotyped forms of letter in the private secretary's office ready for issue to all candidates. When a neatly-written letter in a fine official cover stamped "On Her Majesty's Service," reaches the candidate's address, he finds, not the appointment which he coveted, but an intimation that his name will be inserted in the list of candidates for it, and that the Lieutenant-Governor regrets that he can hold out no immediate hopes, &c. &c. There is sometimes an unfortunate person who treasures a letter of this kind, and is weak enough after a short interval to pay a further visit to the private secretary. The result is that he receives a letter in "our form No. 2," expressing the Lieutenant-Governor's further regret or surprise at his impatience. If he still persists in his visits, he will eventually receive "our form No. 3," in which he is informed that the Lieutenant-Governor must decline to see him or to make any further communication to him, and then at last, perhaps, his eyes are opened, and he may go so far as to blame himself for having given the Lieutenant-Governor so much trouble, when in reality the Lieutenant-Governor has, perhaps, heard little more of him than his name.

But there is another class of applicants for appointments and promotion who cannot be disposed of quite so easily. The members of the sacred Civil Service, of which caste the Lieutenant-Governor is himself the chief, are accustomed to think that it is their special privilege, and a duty to themselves, to represent to the Lieutenant-Governor their own claims and their own peculiar fitness for any desirable appointment that is vacant, or likely to become vacant, for many of them are not at all content to wait till the vacancy actually occurs. The Lieutenant-Governor usually submits himself to the ordeal of seeing these candidates, and though it is often a sad waste of his time, it is not always without its uses, for it sometimes enables him to obtain a closer insight into the character of the applicant, and at the same time to pick up some information about local affairs under a new light. Sometimes the Lieutenant-Governor has a plan of admitting visitors of this class to breakfast, and it becomes an interesting speculation for him during breakfast to guess with what particular object each individual has come. This arrangement has also occasionally the happy effect of disconcerting the visitors themselves. Mr. Smith, who has arrived from some remote part of the country especially to urge his claims to some particular appointment, finds, to his disgust and amazement, that Mr. Robinson, the very man whose rivalry he most feared, has also come down from his district obviously with the same intention. In such a case the Lieutenant-Governor has great opportunities, if he is master of the conversation at his breakfast-table, of operating on the feelings of Smith and Robinson whilst the rest of the company are present. When breakfast is over, the Lieutenant-Governor usually retires to his study, and the visitors who wish for a private interview wait on till their turn comes to be ushered into the great man's presence. We will draw a veil over the scenes which there occur. It is curious to note how strongly the wish is father to the thought, and how each candidate, if cross-examined immediately on his exit from his interview, will be found to have put the construction most favourable to his own desires on the words uttered by the Lieutenant-Governor. Happy is the Lieutenant-Governor who is able to express his meaning clearly and decisively, and at the same time not to wound the susceptibilities of his visitor. But unless the desired appointment has already been promised to another man, it seldom happens that the candidate is willing to persuade himself that he has no chance of success, however kindly and courteously the Lieutenant-Governor may have tried to make this clear to him.

We will pass on to another phase of the Lieutenant-Governor's social influences. As the head of society he is bound to give what are called entertainments—which may be sub-divided into balls, at homes, dinner parties, garden parties, breakfast parties, picnics, &c. The house called Belvedere, which is the Lieutenant-Governor's official residence at Calcutta, is a large straggling edifice, having been built from somewhat small beginnings until the additions have almost entirely superseded the original structure. It is, unfortunately, wrongly placed to the wind as regards the reception rooms, and although the south verandahs are delightfully cool when there is a southerly breeze, the suite of the drawing-room and dining-room and ball-room runs from north to south, and is badly ventilated, so that the heat becomes excessive whenever the rooms are crowded for a ball or any other large party. Each Lieutenant-Governor has added to and altered the building, so that its capacity has increased in greater proportion than its architectural beauty; and yet it still remains for another Lieutenant-Governor to devise an entrance-hall worthy of the rest of the building. But on the occasion of the state balls which the Lieutenant-Governor gives on several suitable dates, there is certainly a very brilliant *coup d'œil* as one looks through the long vista of the rooms thrown open for dancing; and he must be indeed a cynic who cannot enjoy the cool breeze in the south verandah, or the comfortable arrangements on the grand and semi-lighted stone staircase which leads down to the lawn, and to the large pavilions in which supper is sometimes provided, when the time of the year permits. If you are young, and if you have a heart still at liberty, you cannot do better than try and lose it amidst the scented shrubs and plants which surround the cool recesses and sheltered seats so considerately provided for blushing maidens and whispering lovers.

Perhaps some of the most successful entertainments at Belvedere of late years have been the garden-parties held in the afternoon, to which the native nobility and the most influential and wealthy among the Hindoos, Mahomedans, Parsees, Moguls, Burmese, and every other Eastern nationality are invited, in common with all the English ladies and gentlemen of Calcutta. The mixture of Oriental and European costume produces the happiest effect, and exhibits a picturesque scene which could hardly be matched elsewhere. Native gentlemen are rather shy and sensitive, and are always more or less afraid, especially inside a house, of compromising themselves or being somehow compromised, owing to the machinations of the native servants, by contact with some European arrangements of cooking, or other things which are objectionable according to their ideas. But in an open-air garden party they can wander about without any fear of meeting anything that may be offensive to their caste prejudices. It is much to be regretted that, however well-acquainted he may think himself to be with native habits and feelings, it is almost impossible for an English gentleman to be quite sure that there may not be something in his entertainment for the gratification of native gentlemen which, thanks probably to his own servants, may not be misinterpreted or misunderstood by some of them. But, be this as it may, it is rather difficult for the most fastidious native gentleman to take offence when walking up and down the smooth lawns at Belvedere; and if he diverts his course to seek the tea-tables or the other refreshment tents, he can hardly have anyone but himself to blame. It is very seldom that a Hindoo gentleman takes any refreshment, but some of the Mahomedans occasionally indulge in an ice or a cup of tea. It is very unusual for any native ladies to appear at these garden-parties. There are a few Christian convert ladies who come to them, wearing a sort of English costume, which is, unfortunately, not very becoming to them. Some of the native gentlemen bring their pretty grandchildren with them, as has been mentioned in the previous chapter. But the time has not yet come for a native gentleman to bring his wife out on such occasions, although it is noticeable that a native gentleman is usually very willing to be introduced to the English ladies and to shake hands with them. The native gentlemen attach much importance to the shaking of hands, though it is a custom not originally recognised under their own native codes of etiquette. The time is by no means remote when more than one native nobleman of high caste used promptly to wash his hands after shaking hands with an English gentleman, one of his retinue carrying a gold basin and a supply of water to enable his master to get rid of the pollution of the touch of the white man's hand. But we have been informed that one of the last native noblemen who adopted this practice was cured of it by a sensible Englishman, who, on his part, also produced a servant with a basin and water, and deliberately proceeded to wash his hands in the native nobleman's presence. But we must return from this digression, and make our parting bow to the Lieutenant-Governor as we retire with the rest of the gay crowd.

It has been mentioned that the Lieutenant-Governor of Bengal has an official residence at the mountain station of Darjeling. Thirty years ago it was no easy task to reach Darjeling, and in 1857 the Lieutenant-Governor marched up from Calcutta to the foot of the hills with a regular camp, at the rate of about ten miles a day, and the march occupied fully six weeks. But now the railway has altered all this. The Lieutenant-Governor gets into his special train at Calcutta at 4 P.M. on Monday, and by noon on Tuesday he finds himself safely in his mountain residence at Darjeling. A steam tramway now runs right up the mountains, and thus Darjeling is much more accessible than Simla, which is not yet provided with a similar tramway. The principal drawbacks to Darjeling are the heavy rain and the dense mists, which too frequently envelop the whole of the mountain ranges. But when there is a clear and bright day, the view of the everlasting snows, with the mighty Kinchenjunga in all its majesty, is grand and glorious beyond all description. It is, however, rather the fashion for the Lieutenant-Governor and his secretaries, and the other great officials who follow in his train to Darjeling, to make themselves out to be great martyrs to colds and coughs and neuralgia and other maladies, which they attribute to the cold and damp and misty climate of the hills. It seems rather strange that if they dislike the climate so much they should take the trouble to go to Darjeling. But these grumblings are really only lip-deep, and they know very well that it is much more comfortable to sleep in a cool room, with a cheerful fire in it, than to remain down in the plains with the thermometer at 80, and to have to court sleep under the influence of a punkah—which has to be pulled by a native who is unpleasantly prone to go to sleep, and so to cease pulling the punkah.

However, when the rain is heaviest at Darjeling, in July or August, the Lieutenant-Governor and the principal grumblers of his suite take the opportunity to descend to the plains, as this is the time when the Lieutenant-Governor of Bengal can most conveniently proceed on a tour in his state yacht, or barge, to visit some of the remote portions of his province, which are not easily accessible except by water. The state yacht is built something in the shape and style of the Lord Mayor's barge, or one of the house-boats now so common on the Thames, only it is much larger, and it is fitted up with everything that is needed to make it tolerably cool and comfortable, for the temperature in the shade in the rainy season is generally about 80° in Bengal. The yacht is towed by a powerful steamer, and all the cooking is carried on in the steamer, which also conveys all the native servants and official clerks, and the horses and ponies which usually accompany the Lieutenant-Governor on tour. When the yacht is under steam, and going along at about ten or twelve miles an hour, it is exceedingly pleasant to sit on the well-sheltered deck and enjoy the cool breeze. The cabins are all fitted up with punkahs, so that those who have to sit and work in their cabins are duly cared for. The scenery on the rivers is not often very attractive, and as the greater part of the country on both sides of the river is under water, the view may be said to be decidedly monotonous. But, however pleasant and cool it may be during the day, and whilst the yacht is in motion, it is when darkness comes on, and it is time to anchor, that the unpleasant heat begins to assert itself; especially if the wind drops, or is shut off by some inconvenient village on the bank of the river. As soon as the lamps are lighted, it often happens that a plague of insects comes on board, either moths, or odoriferous bugs, or flying earwigs, or an army of large grasshoppers. It is wonderful to what a distance these insects come off from the shore as soon as they see the bright lights of the yacht. Fortunately, the dining-saloon is guarded with wire-gauze blinds, so that it is possible to exclude these pests at dinner-time, otherwise the Lieutenant-Governor would have to dine by daylight, which is the custom for ordinary mortals on board the river-steamers and boats.

When the Lieutenant-Governor's yacht arrives at a civil station or large town, it is a day of great excitement for the inhabitants of all classes and degrees. The principal officials present themselves on board the yacht, and take the Lieutenant-Governor's orders on the programme which they have devised for his entertainment. It is the correct thing for the Lieutenant-Governor to go and inspect all the Government offices and the local jail. There is a sort of mania for inspecting jails, and if there is a local lunatic asylum it is sure to hold a high place in the programme. The inspection of the Government offices is usually a solemn mockery. Most officers of any tact understand the meaning of eye-wash, and everything is externally furbished up so as to look its best. The Lieutenant-Governor is only human, and in reality sees very little below the surface of that which is exhibited to him. If the Lieutenant-Governor is known to be of a cantankerous disposition, as has, unfortunately, been the case sometimes, the proper thing to be done is to lay traps for him, and to present to his eyes something which will at once give him offence; such, for instance, as a treasure-chest with a broken hinge, or a large bundle of old papers all worm-eaten and almost illegible. He will at once fly at these objects, so shocking to his sense of official propriety, and whilst he is fiercely hunting the foxes which have been thus turned out, he will pass blindly by a dozen other things which might really have been worthy of his notice. With an intelligent and kindly Lieutenant-Governor, who understands his business, it is equally safe to proceed on an entirely different plan, and to point out to him the defects and the wants of the place with the full knowledge that he will make due allowance for them. No sensible Lieutenant-Governor is over-anxious to find fault, or to bring discredit on the local officers, who are obviously doing their little best, as he well knows by the recollection of his own experiences in a similar position. It is often a matter of great convenience if the occasion of the Lieutenant-

Governor's visit can be seized, either to lay the foundation stone of some new public building, or to celebrate the completion and opening of some new institution or work of public utility, such as water-works, or a new bridge or hospital. This affords an opportunity for the presentation of an appropriate address, in which the usual platitudes about the development of municipal institutions and the recognition of the capacity of natives for self-government must find their proper place and expression. The richest and most influential native subscribers to the work are then introduced, and on receiving a few kindly words from the Lieutenant-Governor's lips they feel at once certain that they will shortly find themselves authorised in the *Government Gazette* to style themselves C.S.I. or C.I.E., unless a native title is more consonant to their feelings. The principal official of the station then entertains the Lieutenant-Governor and his party at dinner, unless the Lieutenant-Governor takes the precaution to ask all the principal residents to dine on board his yacht, which is by far the safest course for him to adopt. If the Lieutenant-Governor has not a good cook, good food, and good wine with him in his yacht, he is not fit to be Lieutenant-Governor. For in a remote district the best and most liberal local official may have but an indifferent cook, who, perhaps, takes the opportunity to get drunk; and the local supplies of food and wine and ice may not be of the very best quality. Therefore, a Lieutenant-

Governor with due respect for his own health and comfort, does well to invite the local people to dine with him in his yacht, instead of going on shore to dine with them. And after dinner the broad deck of the yacht affords an excellent space for an evening party, to which the Lieutenant-Governor can ask all the other local residents, and especially all the native gentlemen who do not care to be invited to dinner. Probably some wealthy native gentlemen illuminate their houses, or get up a display of fire-works on the river-banks near the yacht; and this counts, in the eyes of the assembled crowds, as part of the evening's entertainment. And so the night wears on, and by the time that the last guest has gone on shore the Lieutenant-Governor has long been slumbering peacefully in his cabin; and the next day, as soon as the rosy-fingered dawn appears, the anchor is weighed, and the steamer and yacht proceed on their journey to some other station, where the Lieutenant-Governor will have again to go through the same kind of business as that which we have attempted to describe. So we will now bid him farewell.

CHAPTER III.

ENGLISH COLONISTS IN BENGAL.

HITHERTO we have written of "kings and tetrarchs and all great things" in India. Now let us go to a different degree in the social scale, to those who were alluded to as the real colonists of India in the first of these chapters. There are now hundreds, or rather thousands, of our countrymen settled in India who may be taken as representing the middle-classes of England; though it might be more correct to use the public-school term, the "upper-middle" classes. Some of these are employed in the cultivation and manufacture of indigo, or sugar, or jute, or other mercantile produce, in the hot and steamy plains of Bengal. Others, who are engaged in the management of tea-gardens, occupy hilly tracts, many of which are as hot and steamy as the plains; though some tea is grown at high altitudes, and in a comparatively cooler climate, as on the mountain-slopes around Darjeling. Others are employed in managing and working the railways which now traverse the length and breadth of the country, and for these there is no escape from all the perils and vicissitudes of the greatest heat. In most of the large towns throughout the country there are established firms of merchants, of which some of the partners are constantly flitting backwards and forwards between India and England, though there is always some local representative of the name and business of the firm left in India. Amongst the trading or shop-keeping classes there are some who have their branch "establishments" at the great hill stations, such as Simla, to which they migrate in order to escape from the heat of the plains when the Court and fashion of the capital retire there with a similar object.

Under the name of colonists we may readily give the first place to those who are engaged in the cultivation aad manufacture of indigo. Owing to circumstances to which we need not further allude, the indigo-planters have not fared well in recent times, especially in some parts of the country, where, to put the case simply, it was no longer possible to grow indigo at a profit, so that the business must have come to an end of itself without the mischievous meddling of agitators, or the irritating intervention of prejudiced Government officials. But there are still many parts of the country, especially in the province of Behar, where indigo may be cultivated successfully; and if the season is favourable, and the crop good, and the London market-price satis-

4

factory, a handsome profit may be made. There are some few indigo-factories or "concerns" which may almost always be trusted year after year to yield a good and profitable out-turn. But it is not by any means a general rule to be so prosperous. At some places either too heavy rain or too little rain may spoil the growing crop. A neighbouring river may overflow its banks and drown all the hopes of the husbandmen, or the much-needed water may refuse to appear in the river at the proper time, so that the well-grown plant cannot be manufactured into the dye. These are but a few out of the many troubles that attend the cultivation of indigo. There are some years when the life of the indigo-planter is a life of mere agony and anxiety, and nothing that his skill or experience can suggest or devise is of the slightest avail to ward off the impending ruin of his crop and of his hopes for a successful season.

But for all this, the life of an indigo-planter is generally healthy and happy, and at all events it is more suited to the taste and disposition of most young Englishmen than the dull routine of a merchant's office or a bank. Let us try to picture to ourselves the buildings and surroundings of the indigo-planter's home. There is a cheerful and substantial house nestling in the shelter of some fine trees; there is a broad lawn, and a flower-garden full of roses and myrtles and variegated flowering shrubs. There is the well-stocked kitchen-garden with its constant supplies of

English vegetables. There are the stables and coach-houses which we may presently inspect. There are the poultry-yards, where no small flock of fowls and ducks and geese and turkeys will be found. The rabbit-hutches are not neglected, and the pigeon-house literally swarms with pigeons. The sleek milch-cows, with their calves, have their appointed places; and you may be sure that there are good kennels for the dogs. A little apart from the dwelling-house the factory-buildings will usually be found, with the vats and apparatus for steeping and pressing the indigo to extract the dye, and the boiling-house with its tall and ugly chimney, and the drying-houses where the cakes of indigo are kept until it is time to pack and despatch them to Calcutta for sale. All the factory-buildings usually stand in one *compound*, as the local term goes, and this is in size almost equal to a small park, surrounded by a high grassy bank or fence to keep off trespassers, and usually studded with some fine groups of trees, in the shade of which the cattle take shelter from the mid-day heat. The English colonist is ever anxious to keep up the appearance of a comfortable English home, and not merely the appearance but the solid substance, so far as the difference of climate permits.

An indigo factory is usually managed by one of the owners or partners in the concern. Let us take the case of a healthy hardy man a little past thirty years of age, who has served an apprenticeship of several years as an assistant in the factory of which he at length stands forth as manager. He has acquired a certain share as part-owner in the factory, and will thus earn his quota in the profits of the season, whilst he has a separate fixed salary and sundry emoluments in his special capacity as manager. His position is thoroughly independent, if so be that he and his partners have sufficient capital of their own to carry on the expenditure of the concern. If they have not the requisite capital, their agents in Calcutta finance the concern, making such advances as are needed for the purchase of seed, the cost of cultivation, payment of rents, and all the other expenses which must be provided for until the produce of the season can be sold and brought to account. The profitable condition of an indigo factory depends chiefly on the capacity of the owners to provide their own funds, or on their having to borrow them. For as the cultivation is precarious, and the amount of the produce varies from year to year, money cannot be borrowed on such security except at a heavy charge for interest. With commission and other charges the borrower has to pay about twenty per cent. for the capital which he borrows. Of course, it makes a very great difference at the end of the season if twenty per cent. has to be deducted from the net profits of the concern.

At certain times of the year the indigo planter has rather a hard-worked life. In what may be termed the spring-time, when the plant is growing, he must be up with the dawn for a long ride through the fields to see that the cultivators are looking properly after their work. The hot and blazing sun rises, but he heeds it little, as his anxious eyes are bent on noting any changes for good or bad that may have occurred in the crop since he last rode in this direction. He does not, however, disdain the shelter of a friendly tree, if so be that his course is arrested by a party of anxious villagers who seek his advice or orders about the right to use some water for irrigation, or to fish in some particular pond, or to settle some minute question of caste—such, for instance, as the grave question whether some new arrival is entitled to be shaved by the village barber. I have sat for more than an hour with a planter listening to all the earnest arguments submitted for his decision on this point. Sometimes also, his ride may be interrupted by less peaceable demonstrations, for an aggressive neighbour may have trespassed on his cultivated lands, or he may find a hostile force arrayed to prevent him from ploughing certain fields to which he considers himself entitled. Fortunately the stand-up fights of armed retainers, which were not uncommon years ago, are now almost unknown, and those who are wisest in their generation now are careful to avoid any recourse to force in settling their disputes with their neighbours. At length the morning round is finished, and he gallops home through the fiery sunshine, giving his horse the benefit of a little practice at a few jumps over any banks and ditches that lie conveniently in his path.

As he rides up to his house the children and the "placens uxor" appear, probably to chide him for being so late out in the hot sun, as it seems to be the first duty of a good wife always to remind her husband that he ought to take more care of himself. Probably, however, the lady is anxious for her breakfast; whilst the children, who have had their breakfast, are only too glad to welcome their father and to follow him into his dressing-room to have their little talk with him, and to watch all the mysterious operations of dressing which seem to have such a fascination for children. In India each little child of two or three years old has its own special man or boy servant in charge of it, so that the children can be still cared for in their father's dressing-room, which might be not quite so convenient in England, where children are in charge of nurses. But when their father has bathed and dressed, the children lead him out into the breakfast-room, and, probably having got some spoil from the breakfast-table, they retire to their mid-day slumbers and are seen no more.

The mid-day breakfast at a factory is usually one of the most pleasant hours of the day. The friends who are staying in the house, for planters are very hospitable, and any neighbours (neighbours meaning people living within twenty miles) who have come over for a morning visit, all present themselves at the well-decked table. It is hardly necessary to say that breakfast at 12 o'clock indicates that there is to be no lunch at 1 or 2 o'clock, and it is, in fact, breakfast and lunch combined. Therefore, the dishes are both numerous and serious; and as the sun is over the yard-arm, in nautical phrase, the men have fully earned their right to a draught of cool beer, or of claret or hock with such combinations of soda and iced materials as the heart desires. When a man has been in the saddle for several hours with a fine blazing sun overhead, and the temperature almost beyond the thermometer's power of measurement, it is not astonishing that a good pull at a tankard of beer is something like a fabulous draught of nectar. It is a sort of medical axiom that as long as a man can take plenty of outdoor exercise in India, he can drink as much beer as is good for him; and *vice versâ*, if he wishes to drink beer he must be careful to take plenty of exercise. But to some constitutions beer is always hostile, and so they must have recourse to claret, or hock, or burgundy; or it may be brandy and soda, but this is always to be shunned as much as possible. However, breakfast must come to an end; and when the ladies of the house retire to the drawing-room, the men usually take their arm-chairs and a pipe, and not unfrequently the conversation gradually drops, until they have all quietly passed off into a gentle doze, which is nature's best restorer at this hour of the day.

But it is not to be supposed that the planter's work is now at an end. He must rouse himself after forty winks, and go off to his cutcherry or office, where he must pass a few hours in company with his native clerks and subordinates. His work is usually interesting and diversified. He must look to his letters from his Calcutta agents, who want to be kept well posted up as to the prospects of the coming crop, and the various heads of expenditure for which money has to be provided. There are communications more or less friendly or unfriendly from the district officials in whose courts civil or criminal suits are pending on behalf of or against people connected with the factory. However peaceably disposed a planter may be, some of his neighbours or some of his own people are sure to bring him before the courts in some way. He may have to receive a visit from his wealthy native neighbour, who has come with sweet words in his mouth, but whose heart is full of bitterness and war. He must listen to the complaints of his own people, and he must sometimes minister to their physical complaints also, though at most large factories a regular medical establishment is maintained to provide for those who are sick or suffering from accidental injuries. As a matter of fact, also, an influential planter administers justice in a quiet way among his own people, and prevents them, if he can, from taking their petty quarrels and disputes into the Government courts, where the expenses of litigation are often almost ruinous to the poorer classes. And thus it comes to pass that the planter finds plenty of occupation in his office for several hours in the afternoon, and he is only too glad when he receives a message from his wife to say that the carriages and horses are ready for the evening drive, or that he is expected to come forth to take his part in a game of polo or lawn-tennis.

Planters are always hospitable. In India it is a sort of maxim still that the guest confers the favour, for, of course, the guest is really very welcome when your nearest neighbour lives five miles from you. And so each planter gathers round him from time to time a little party of visitors and neighbours, and when the men are sufficiently numerous they get up a game of polo. Perhaps the best social game that was ever invented for India was Badminton, which has now been almost superseded by lawn-tennis. Badminton has never been much appreciated in England; but in India the absence of high wind and rain was much in its favour, and there were many ladies who played it almost as well as men. For, as was well said by a learned judge, men and women are almost on an equality as regards the upper part of their dress, and can use their hands and heads with nearly equal effect. But when a lawn-tennis ball makes a bound into the skirts of a lady's dress she has not the same facility of escaping from it as her male adversary. Therefore, as the shuttlecock of Badminton was always flying high, and from head to head, so to speak, Badminton for a long time in India held its own against the introduction of lawn-tennis; though the day has come now when lawn-tennis has ousted its old opponent, and both ladies and men look forward to their game of lawn-tennis as soon as it is possible to find a court sheltered sufficiently by shady trees against the rays of the declining sun. The temperature may be above 80°, but, nevertheless, bright-faced and neatly-dressed girls come out arrayed for the combat, and thinking little of the heat and the fatigue if they can only get good partners and a good game. Those who are accustomed to judge of Indian ladies only from their pale and worn countenances when they return invalided to England, would hardly believe with what vigour and spirit the same ladies played lawn-tennis in India as long as their health and strength lasted.

When darkness puts an end to the play there is no lack of refreshment suited to the taste of each sex, and there are some men who are so selfish that they do not scruple to light their cigars and pipes in the presence of the ladies, but it is to be regretted that the good old fashion has passed away when no man smoked in the presence of a lady. Certainly the men have plenty of advantages special to themselves. For instance, when the ladies have to go into the house to prepare for dinner and change their dresses, the men usually adjourn to the swimming-bath. At many large factories there is a fine swimming-bath in a house built for the purpose, from 50 to 70 feet long, and more than half as wide. One of the greatest pleasures of which the human body is capable is to plunge hissing-hot into the clear and cool water of the bath, and to swim a few lazy strokes to the nearest resting-place. There used to be a medical myth, that it was dangerous for a man to bathe when very hot. But later and wiser doctors have discovered the error, and very grateful we should be for their discovery. To those who have learnt at Eton, or elsewhere, to take a good "header" we can recommend no more exquisite sensation than that which they will derive from plunging red hot into the cool water of a swimming-bath.

There may be more splendid entertainments elsewhere, but there are few more sociable and pleasant dinner-parties than those which crown the labours of the day at a good indigo-factory. The ladies are not often quite equal in number to the men; but that is a fault on the right side so far as they are concerned, as they will receive all the more attention, whilst there are always one or more greedy or hungry men who are more inclined to devote themselves to the substance of their dinner than to the pleasures of conversation; nor are they absolutely in the wrong. The dishes may be simple, but they are sure to be good. Who does not remember the saddle of mutton from a sheep reared and carefully fed in the farm up to its fourth year? Neither the downs of Sussex nor the hills of Wales produce more delicate and well-flavoured meat. What is there to be compared with the whiteness and tenderness of the well-boiled capon, the last fortnight of whose life has been the subject of the most careful feeding, as he passed, day by day, through the separate compartments of the fattening range until he was promoted to the condemned cell at the head of the range? Capons should, of course, be well fed always, but for the last fortnight they should be taken up and fed most delicately in a fattening range specially constructed with fourteen or fifteen compartments with sliding panels between them, so that those who are being thus treated for about a fortnight, find themselves promoted day by day towards the highest compartment, a condemned cell, from which there is no promotion except to the kitchen. We cannot stop to enumerate all the fine vegetables, such as the potatoes which have been grown in a soil prepared with the refuse stalks of the indigo plant, which is most congenial to them, so that no better potatoes ever came out of Ireland. There are champion peas from Sutton's best seed. There is celery equal to the best that England can exhibit. We will not even notice the better kinds of Indian vegetables; but the dinner is by no means a dinner of herbs, and those who have come to it with good appetite and good digestion are not likely to go empty away. Early hours are the rule at a factory, and when the men have joined the ladies in the drawing-room a little music may sometimes be supplemented by a little dancing; but as a rule most of the party are not unwilling to seek their bed-rooms, with the knowledge that they have to rise on the morrow with the early dawn, either for the renewal of their daily labour or to return to their own houses.

> Quis non malarum quas amor curas habet
> Hæc inter obliviscitur?

Doubtless there can scarcely be a more enjoyable life than that of a successful and healthy indigo-planter. But there must be at times a darker side to the picture. Illness may break out suddenly, and before any skilled medical aid can arrive the hand of death may have robbed the household of one of its darlings. We all know with what fearful rapidity cholera seizes on its victims, and when once cholera has marked a house it is seldom content with only one victim. Some of the numerous domestic servants are almost sure to take alarm, and to frighten themselves into the belief that they must die. It is an anxious and awful time. Nor are other minor dangers and alarms wanting. In some factories it is almost impossible to keep cobras and other dangerous snakes from coming into the house; and many a parent has found a deadly cobra in painful proximity to the pillow of a child sleeping happily unconscious of its danger, but liable to put itself in peril by the slightest movement. Or, whilst the master is still out on his morning rounds, the affrighted servants rush to their mistress with the news that a mad dog or a mad jackal is running about the garden, and has attacked and scared the gardeners. But it is useless to multiply instances. Fortunately, the larger animals of prey are no longer to be found in the district in which indigo is cultivated; but in the tea gardens, which are in the wilder and more jungly parts of the country, even a tiger is an occasional visitor, and leopards are constantly on the watch to carry off a pet dog, or a goat, or a calf from almost under the eyes of the planter.

It would be but an imperfect sketch of the planter-colonist's social life if we did not give some account of the great annual festive gatherings which are held by them at the race meetings at Sonepore and other favourite places. It will be sufficient to take Sonepore as an example, as it is the oldest established meeting, and also is larger and more cosmopolitan (if such a big word is permissible) than other race-meetings, and is the trysting place where the planters of several districts can best assemble. It is not very easy to convey to an English reader an idea of a Sonepore meeting except as a large picnic which lasts for about ten days. But the picnicers do not return to their homes at the end of each day; they live on the spot in tents which are gathered together in separate camps, or parties, or messes; so that independently of the general picnic life of the whole assemblage, there are wheels within wheels, and each separate camp or mess carries on its own picnic on its own independent and self-supporting arrangements. The ostensible primary object of the Sonepore meeting is a race-meeting, but it is also intimately connected with, and based upon, the large Native Fair which is held simultaneously with it, to which we shall presently recur. The race-course runs round a flat plain rather larger perhaps than the space enclosed by the course at Ascot or Epsom. Almost all round the outside of the race-course there are groves of mango trees not quite so stately as the horse-chestnuts of Bushey Park, or the elms of the Long Walk at Windsor, but fine old trees of considerable height, and with a thick green foliage that affords a grateful shade against the rays of the sun. Underneath these groves of mango trees, stretching for nearly a mile along the east side of the course, the several camps are formed. Each camping-ground has its well-defined boundaries and is rented from year to year. One camp belongs to the young Hindoo Rajah of Durbanga, who was lately the chief supporter of the races. In fact he may be said to have two camps, one for his native friends, and one for his English friends. The Government officials of the several neighbouring districts have their separate or combined camps. Sometimes the Viceroy of India has had a camp, and sometimes the Lieutenant-Governor has sent over his tents for the meeting. The regiments from the nearest military station have their own camps and messes, with their bands to discourse sweet music. The planters of the several districts have either joint or separate camps according to their numbers and strength, and they rival one another in hospitality. The tents of each camp are arranged as far as possible in a square of which one side is open and facing the road that runs through the grove of trees. The mess tent of each camp is pitched at the further side from the entrance, and in front of it there is usually a huge awning (called in native parlance a shamyana) which serves as an *al fresco* drawing-room, comfortably arranged with couches and arm-chairs, and big Persian carpets and rugs, and other appliances. Each camp usually contains its own Badminton courts and its lawn-tennis court, if the trees will allow sufficient space. At the back of the mess-tent there come the cooking-tents and the tents for the servants, as well as for the horses and carriages of the party. Each camp is guarded by a party of native watchmen, who have the credit of being hereditary thieves, but are scrupulously honest for the occasion as regards the contents of the camp committed to their care which they are well paid to watch. But woe betide the self-sufficient stranger who dispenses with the services of these watchmen, confiding in his own prowess and the services of his own retainers.

The race-meeting at Sonepore usually takes place in November, when the weather is beginning to be really cool and pleasant. It is regulated by some native festival, much as the Derby day is dependent on the date of Easter. As the time approaches the stewards of the meeting take measures to have the race-stand and ball-room swept and garnished, and the camping-grounds and race-course put in proper order. A few days before the meet, trains of country bullock-carts may be seen approaching the ground laden with the ponderous tents, and beds and chairs and tables, and every kind of furniture that is needed for civilised life. Nor is the commissariat likely to be forgotten, whilst those who can manage it conveniently, send over their own cows to supply milk and butter, and the fatlings of the flock, and huge baskets and coops full of turkeys and geese and poultry. Ponderous deal boxes full of Fortnum and Masonry, and cases labelled with the names of the most promising brands of champagne and hock, and the well-known six-dozen chests of beer, with heavy supplies of soda and seltzer, occupy many of the carts. It is quite a study to see how skilfully the native servants get everything into order before their masters' arrival; especially the cook, who at once sets to work and extemporises a mud kitchen, on which during the next week he will perform culinary wonders, although it may be well for the fastidious not to pry too narrowly into all his proceedings, but to live in faith and satisfy themselves with results.

As the races are the ostensible object of the meeting, all the arrangements are made with special reference to them. There are usually four days' races, on alternate days, *i.e.* on Tuesday, Thursday, and Saturday, and the ensuing Tuesday. The races take place at seven in the morning. Thus most of the visitors arrive on Monday, and on Monday evening the first lotteries are held for speculation on the races which are to take place on Tuesday morning. On Tuesday evening there is a ball;

on Wednesday everyone is supposed to be recovering from the effects of the combined dissipation of Tuesday's races and ball; until Wednesday evening provides another lottery for speculation on the races of Thursday morning, which are to be followed by another ball on Thursday night; so that theoretically a day of rest comes in between each day of pleasure, or "trouble" as the Yankees more rightly call it.

We will attempt to describe the proceedings of one day at Sonepore. It is the first Tuesday, and we are startled from our sleep by the bang of a big cannon, which seems to be at the door of our tent. This is called "gunfire," and means that dawn is breaking. Just as you are composing yourself to sleep again you hear the sound of music, and there comes the band of a native regiment playing some noisy tune as they march along the road through the centre of all the camps, and, having got to the end of it, back they come again playing louder than before. Meanwhile all the servants have been aroused, and your man comes into the tent and tells you that it is time to get up; and, in fact, unless you mean to cut the amusement altogether, it is best to get up and dress. By the time you reach your camp mess-tent you will probably find the charming hostess who presides over your camp ready and waiting for you with one or two of her pretty girls, whose fresh and bright faces never look better than at this early and trying time. Tea and coffee are ready for you, and, as the party gradually collects in the tent, the carriages come to the entrance of the camp, and you either drive to the race-stand, or join a walking party with those who want the little walk to warm them. The race-stand commands a good view of the races; but one race is very much like another, except that at an Indian race-course you probably know most of the owners of the horses, or some of the gentleman-riders, so that a stronger personal feeling exists; and the young ladies will insist on betting for gloves and backing the worst horse in the race, merely because it is to be ridden by that good-looking young officer to whom they are engaged for at least three dances at the coming ball. The races usually last till about 10 o'clock, when we all go back to our camps and make ready for breakfast.

In the hospitable camp to which I belonged for several years at Sonepore, the tea and coffee of breakfast were usually followed or superseded by "just one glass of champagne to begin with," as our kind host would cheerfully say, and it seemed to be generally considered that a few glasses of good champagne were very acceptable at breakfast after the early morning's work. After breakfast no one seems to think of repose. Some of the younger people at once set to work at Badminton and lawn-tennis; others make up parties to go to see the horses and elephants, and other sights of the native fair; whilst others set forth to pay visits at the other camps, for there is a sort of unwritten law of etiquette that all the camps should call on one another as fast as possible. By 2 o'clock we are summoned to lunch, and again the champagne flows freely for those who prefer it to beer or other liquids. After lunch the hostess of the camp usually tries to get some of the ladies to rest themselves in their tents, on the plea of looking after their dresses for the ball in the evening; but there are some perverse and indefatigable girls who will go on with lawn-tennis, or join in a Badminton tournament, until tea is announced. Then the carriages and horses come to the door, and we all drive or ride out to the course. There is probably a fierce game of polo going on between civil and military, or the planters of two rival districts, or the Public Schools against the World, or any other combination of forces that can be devised. On some days there are cricket-matches arranged between similar parties and factions. Meanwhile one of the military bands is playing in front of the race-stand, and there pour forth upon the course all the carriages and horses that can be mustered for the occasion. There are a few ladies riding with their attendant squires. There comes the drag of the young Raja of Durbanga covered with his lady guests, whilst the Raja himself handles the reins and puts his well-broken horses into a gallop along the back of the course. Tandems driven from high dog-carts seem to have a special attraction for some young ladies, and after the horses have steadied down a little to their work, the reins are usually transferred to the hands of the young lady until some impending danger makes it necessary to resume them from her. However, collisions and accidents rarely occur; and as darkness speedily comes on, the carriages and their occupants soon disappear from the course and return to their camps.

About 8 o'clock the camp-gong gives the signal for dinner, and a party of about twenty or thirty assemble in almost every mess-tent. In a well-managed camp the hostess generally takes care to fill up any vacancies at her table by inviting guests from the other camps. Any member of a camp who is going out to dinner is expected to give early notice to his hostess, so that she may be able to ask a friend from some other camp in his place. By this arrangement an agreeable exchange of hospitality is kept up, and the monotony of always having the same set of faces avoided. Many of the ladies appear at dinner ready dressed for the ball afterwards, but some of the most wary ones reserve a few final touches of dress for after dinner. It is astonishing what a magic effect is sometimes produced by those few final touches. It is hardly necessary to say that during dinner much fun and merriment prevail all round the table. However the guests may be told off and assorted at first, it is curious to observe how, after a day or two, certain young ladies and certain young gentlemen always happen to sit next or near to one another at the several meals, and take a sort of monopoly of certain seats for themselves and their own particular acquaintances. It not seldom happens that some unfortunate youth makes himself ridiculous or in some way obnoxious to the other young people, and then they all combine to make his life a burthen to him unless he shows symptoms of reformation and better behaviour. Of course, long before dinner the ball-cards of all the best dancers are filled up, but during dinner a half promise of one more " extra " may be secured, or some convenient exchange of promised dances arranged to suit the wishes of sisters or bosom friends. But we must not linger too long over the dinner-table. The carriages are announced to be ready, and are rapidly filled and sent off to the ball-room, from which sometimes they come back to be refilled by a second detachment of the party.

The ball-room at Sonepore is a well-proportioned room which holds about two hundred people conveniently. The music is provided by the regimental bands in turns, and is usually very good. A long verandah and corridor outside the ball-room, not too brilliantly lighted up, afford a convenient retreat for those who wish to improve the opportunities of the dance by a little further conversation with their partner before she returns to her chaperone, or is carried off by the man to whom she is engaged for the next dance. If you wander along the corridor you will come first to the tea-room, and then to the supper-room, which will not be opened before midnight. Dancing is usually kept up with much spirit; and as there are always more gentlemen than ladies, the latter seldom have to sit out a dance for want of a partner. But, of course, one ball is very like another ball, and they must all come to an end. Some prudent mammas insist on going away before supper, others more indulgently remain throughout the whole of the programme; but at last "God save the Queen" admonishes even the latest lingerers that it is time to go home. We must not follow the young ladies to their tents; but it is very well known that they do sit up there for a very long time, laughing and talking over all the incidents of the ball. To the men the hour after the ball is often one of grateful refreshment, as we gather together in the comfortable armchairs of the *al fresco* drawing-room, and sit wrapped in our great-coats, smoking the fragrant weed, and protecting ourselves from the cold night air with steaming glasses of whisky-and-water, and discussing the events of the day and the plans of the morrow, until we retreat to our tents comforted with the knowledge that there will be no big gun fired to wake us at daybreak, and there will be no horrid band marching through the camp to disturb our slumbers. And so end the labours of a long Tuesday.

Wednesday is theoretically to be a day of rest. The camp breakfast hour is fixed at 10, but there are some ardent spirits who know no repose, and your rest is disturbed by the noise made in the adjacent tent by your friends Jones and Smith, who are bent on an expedition to shoot snipe or quail before breakfast. Other men are getting up early to go down to the fair to look at the horses which are for sale; and presently the soft voices of fair girls are heard, and you find that two or more of them have emerged from their tents to have just one game of lawn tennis before breakfast, by way of practice for the impending tournament. How delightful it must be to be young and not to know what fatigue means! And so this theoretical day of rest goes on. After breakfast every sort of amusement is arranged for the day, and no one seems to think of resting. One of the things that has to be done at Sonepore is to go and see the native fair. It is most convenient to go to the fair on an elephant, as the crowds of people are so dense, and many of the roads at the fair are too narrow, or otherwise unsuited for carriages. So two or three elephants are brought round, and parties made up to mount them. There is usually room for about four persons on each elephant; and if two young men can find themselves on an elephant with two pretty girls, they seem to think themselves in the seventh heaven. The movements of an elephant are sometimes rather rough, and the fair riders not only hold on desperately at first to the ropes, but seldom object to be also held on by the stronger arm of man. However, away they go, jolting and swaying about under the trees, and trying to manage their umbrellas or parasols so as to keep off the sun, which still smites down fiercely with his rays. As we arrive at the native fair, we first come upon endless rows of horses tethered under the long ranges of trees.

The horses are numbered by hundreds, or rather by thousands, and come from the most distant parts of India, and sometimes from Bokhara and Persia; some of them look very handsome with their arched necks and long manes. But we must not detain our fair charges here too long. Onwards we go, a large bell round the elephant's neck warning the swarming crowd to keep out of the way. The fair is laid out in the usual Oriental style, with all the vendors of one sort of thing collected in one place, or bazaar, as it is called. Here is the shoe bazaar, with fifty little shops or stalls, full of every kind of leather shoe of native make, and the gayest slippers embroidered with gold thread, and also a small stock of patent-leather shoes of English make to suit the tastes of those who have been educated to consider a patent-leather shoe as emblematic of an acquisition of a knowledge of English. Next we come to the cloth bazaar, where, in another fifty shops, all the manufactures of Manchester are to be seen, either in the original bales, or opened out and temptingly displayed to attract customers. The next bazaar is full of shops containing eatables, not eatables suited to the English taste, but different sorts of rice and and grains, and confections of sugar and almonds and cocoa-nuts and pastry, in which our native brethren delight. At a corner where two roads cross, and the crowd is densest, you will find an English or American missionary mounted on a chair, and addressing the multitude with a vehemence and earnestness which arrests their attention for a few moments, but, unfortunately, seldom produces any permanent results. Presently we come to the place where the dealers in elephants keep these animals for sale, and we pass among these rather dangerous monsters with some apprehension, lest a sudden fit of jealousy or excitement should make some irascible "Jumbo" attack our elephant. Hundreds of elephants are standing about in groups under the trees, whilst others are being taken down to bathe in the neighbouring river. Onward we go, to find ourselves amongst long strings of camels. Then we come to the police encampment, where the native officer in charge of the arrangements of the fair has provided a temporary lock-up for offenders; but offences are usually very few and trivial. Next we come to the bazaar where the sounds of music may be heard from morn till night, and through the long hours of the night; whilst nautch-girls dance and sing for the delectation of their native audience, who sit for hours like enchanted listeners. Finally, let us visit the bird-bazaar, where all kinds of fancy birds are collected, parrots of all sorts in hundreds, peacocks, quails, bulbuls, talking mynas, Java sparrows, and hundreds of other pretty feathered creatures. At length it is time to return to camp, and we wend our way back under the trees, weary and dusty, and grateful that our elephant has not walked over any of the hundreds of thousands of our Aryan brethren amongst whom we have been wandering. We alight from the elephant, feeling rather happy to be released from the back-breaking position; and, after exhibiting the wonderful bargains and purchases which we have made, we hasten to prepare ourselves for the pleasures of lunch and some well-iced refreshing drink.

It would be tedious to go on with a repetition of the daily laborious round of pleasure and enjoyment which lasts for the ten days of the meeting. We have only space to allude to one special form of pleasure, viz. the camp-fire evenings, for which Sonepore is particularly famous. The officers of the English regiment usually issue an invitation for a camp-fire party after dinner, with their band to play; or they kindly lend their band to some other camp which may have a larger and more convenient space for a good camp-fire. A huge bonfire is then piled up in the centre of the space before the camp, and when the torch is applied it blazes up fiercely, whilst all the guests sit round on chairs and couches and listen to the music of the band. Sometimes a few songs and glees are sung. It is a weird but charming scene as we look round on all the quaint figures wrapped up in shawls and cloaks and great-coats and extemporised head-dresses; for it is just cold enough to make a few warm garments acceptable, though there is no great risk of catching cold in the calm and soft night air. There is certainly something almost savouring of the supernatural which comes over the mind at these camp-fire evenings, and it is well known that many a fair maiden has found the time and place not unsuitable to receive the confession of undying love and affection which her youthful admirer had previously hesitated to make. It may be that the bonfire was burning low; but when it suddenly blazes out again with fresh and bright flames, watchful eyes are not wanting to observe how by some casual movement the unsuspecting young pair have come into a proximity which obviously indicates that a great and happy change has suddenly come over their future destiny.

No one who has been at a Sonepore race-meeting can ever forget the pleasures, in so many new and varied forms, which he there enjoyed. The life in the open air under the shady trees, the perfect liberty of the friendly interchange of hospitality, the cordial greetings of old friends, the pleasant introductions to new acquaintances, all throw a special charm over the reminiscences of it. It is not to be wondered at that by the planters of the adjoining districts, and also by the Government officials, the Sonepore meeting is looked forward to as the great event of the year. As soon as one meeting is half over, plans and engagements are entered into with a view to prepare for the enjoyment of the meeting of the coming year. Let us hope that these meetings may long continue to flourish; and if any of my old hosts were to send a very pressing invitation to me, I am half-inclined to think that I would go out all the way from England to India to take advantage of it.

CHAPTER IV.

THE BENGAL CIVIL SERVICE.

Lord Ellenborough, once Governor-General of India, and formerly President of the Board of Control, records in his political diary how the Duke of Wellington always mentioned in high terms the gallantry of the Indian army and the purity of the Civil Service. We must leave it to others to write of the Indian army. For the present we propose to devote our attention to the Civil Service in its extensive social relations in India. The purity of the Civil Service may well be said to be its distinguishing characteristic; and for this quality it was specially held in honour by the great Duke. The pure light of the Civil Service of India still shines like a guiding star before the faces of the millions of our Oriental subjects and allies.

And yet there are many people in England who have much to learn about the Indian Civil Service.

They have heard of the Civil Service Supply Association in London, and they know that it is managed by the Civil Servants of the Government public offices in London, who are fully entitled to call themselves the Civil Servants of the Crown. In a single year about 15,000 candidates compete for the Home Civil Service, and about 5,000 are passed. Their name is legion, and they pervade the whole country. But the Indian Civil Service is a much more select and exclusive service. Only about forty new candidates are admitted to it by competitive examination each year. These are the recruits who are sent out annually to replenish the Civil Service throughout the whole of India in the three Presidencies of Bengal, Bombay, and Madras, and their dependencies. There are less than 1,000 members of the Civil Service in the whole of India. In the lower provinces of Bengal, to which this article is chiefly devoted, the Civil Service consisted recently of only 255 members. It is but a little leaven to leaven the whole mass of the native population of Lower Bengal, which numbers more than sixty millions according to the last census.

It is no easy task to attempt to describe the duties of the Indian Civil Service. As to the Indian civilian himself, the pen might almost hesitate to describe him. It reminds us of the epitaph on a good wife—

> She was, but words are wanting to say what.
> Think what a wife should be, and she was that.

It would perhaps be easier to say what an Indian

civilian should be than what he is. He should be not less capable and omniscient than the late Lord John Russell, prepared to command the Channel fleet, or to perform an operation in lithotomy. There is a story current of a distinguished civilian in the mutinies of 1857–58 to whom Lord Clyde said, "Why, Mr. P., you seem to wish to command the army." "And a very laudable ambition too, I think, my Lord," replied Mr. P., unabashed. The government of a province and its millions of inhabitants is avowedly the ultimate aim and object of each civilian's official life; but whilst he is serving his apprenticeship for the higher offices of Government, he must be prepared to adapt his mind to the most humble and unintellectual duties. He must learn to obey, so that he may understand how to rule. He will have to look after the scavengers who are occupied with the drainage and sanitation of the town in which he lives. He will have to count and deliver out postage-stamps with his own hands, and woe betide him if his treasury accounts and cash balances do not agree to the uttermost farthing. The capacity of a civilian's mental power should be similar to that of the elephant's trunk, which can pick up a pin and pull down a mighty forest tree. There is nothing too great, and hardly anything too small, to which he may not in the course of his career be expected to apply himself.

The civilian is not unfrequently described in the local newspapers as a Celestial official. There is a linguistic basis for this epithet Celestial. Where the Sanskrit and Bengali languages prevail, the civilian is usually addressed by the title of Dhurmavatar, or Incarnation of Justice. Where the Persian and Hindustani languages are more in vogue, he is usually styled Khudawand, which may be translated as "Lord" or "God." The civilian from his official cradle being thus addressed as a superhuman personage, not unnaturally sucks in the high-sounding titles and mentally feeds upon them. What wonder, then, if he unconsciously begins to think with thoughts that are not as those of ordinary mortal men. And thus it comes to pass that the young members of the Civil Service, nurtured on sweet words and addressed continually by flattering and exaggerated titles, surrounded from day to day by suppliant and subservient attendants, and frequently cut off from any direct communication with English friends, do acquire a manner of thought and speech which may strike the non-official observer as savouring of the superhuman or Celestial type. It is unwholesome for the human mind to live in an atmosphere of flattery and honeyed words. We remember a native gentleman of high rank and position who asked for an appointment in a Government office for one of his younger sons. "He is a good lad," he said, "but I want to get him placed where he will find himself addressed by some title less than Maharajah, as he now hears himself called by all the servants on my establishment."

A member of the Civil Service was formerly bound by a covenant to serve the East India Company for the best part of his life. He now enters into a covenant to serve the Queen-Empress of India for a similar term of years. There is a great gulf between the covenanted and uncovenanted servants of the Queen, but at present we can only treat of the covenanted man. In "vulgar parlance" he used to be described as an individual worth £300 a year dead or alive, and this is still his specific social valuation. If he dies and leaves a widow, she will receive from the Civil Fund an annual sum of £300 a year. If whilst he lives he falls into trouble or sickness, he is still entitled by his covenant to a subsistence allowance of £300 a year. He may be, and usually is, a much larger partaker in the pecuniary advantages of his service. But the time was when in the matrimonial market of Calcutta the solid advantages of the covenanted young civilian might thus be weighed against the brilliant uniforms and ever-willing swords of his military rivals; and if the young man owned a buggy, and a silver teapot, and had subscribed to the Civil Fund, he was looked on as eligible for immediate wedlock.

Under the competitive system of admission to the Civil Service, the civilian is now such a very superior person in ability and acquirements, that we will not attempt to describe him. But we will first refer to the men of the old school, before the competitive system was invented and applied to the Indian Civil Service.

We will look back to the time when the civilian in the earliest stage of his Indian career was a most important factor in the fashionable world of Calcutta. Forty or fifty years ago the young civilian, on landing in India, was entered as a student in the College of Fort William. He had passed through the course of instruction and examinations of the old college at Hertford and Haileybury. Discipline at those institutions is said to have been sufficiently lax and irregular. But it was required by the ruling authorities of India that the young civilian, on arriving in India, should again submit himself to some sort of college discipline whilst he was studying the native languages of India in Calcutta. A fine range of buildings called Writers' Buildings represented the Calcutta College. A young civilian was in those times styled a Writer. His appointment was called a Writership. This was an inheritance of the mercantile nomenclature of the East India Company. The Calcutta College owed its constitution and existence in a great measure to the classical theories of the great Marquis of Wellesley when Governor-General of India. But classical theories combined with Oriental developments are calculated to produce a somewhat hybrid progeny. The young civilians landed in India with a not unjustifiable notion of their own personal and social importance. On leaving their English college, the Chairman of the Court of Directors had solemnly addressed them on the dignity and responsibility of their position. They had been informed that they were to be the future governors of India; they had been told that it was their duty to demean themselves as Christian gentlemen, to become a light to the heathen, and the leaders of Oriental civilisation. Is it then a matter of wonder that these young men on arriving in Calcutta found it somewhat difficult to submit themselves again to anything having the name or the appearance of college or scholastic discipline? Be it remembered that each young man on his arrival in India was entitled to an income equivalent to nearly four hundred pounds a year. A gentleman commoner at an English university with £400 a year and confiding tradesmen to give him credit, is not usually found a good subject for discipline. What, then, could be expected from the young men in Calcutta, with a salary of £400 a year, and open access to the purses of every wealthy money-lender in the country? Nor was this all. The Government, aware of the danger of the native money-lender's fatal influence, endeavoured to anticipate and avert it. Each young civilian, whilst in college in Calcutta, was authorised to borrow a sum of £400 from Government. The object of this benevolence was to prevent him from getting into the clutches of the native money-lenders. What was the result? The taste of blood is said to lead to the appetite for more. The young man who had found a loan of £400 almost forced on him by a paternal Government, experienced no difficulty in borrowing several thousand pounds from the native money-lender, who, it may be said, felt confident that the Government would eventually see that he was repaid. The wildest extravagance naturally resulted from this system. The nabob who in the plenitude of his acquired wealth ordered "more curricles," was practically outdone by the young civilian who, with a nominal income of £400 a year, maintained an establishment in Calcutta in which he would not allow the Arab horses in his stable to be counted. He seldom had less than forty horses, but he considered it unlucky to count them. This officer rose subsequently to the highest eminence in the service, and not only paid all his debts, but acquired a respectable competency. A cousin of this gentleman, who also achieved the highest official honours, had a similar love for horses. He had a stud of English race-horses and an English jockey in charge of them. It would be easy but tedious to enumerate other splendid examples of youthful extravagance. It was the fashion to get in debt to the amount of a lakh of rupees, or £10,000, before leaving college. The cautious and canny young man who did not condescend to borrow the £400 proffered to him by Government, was looked upon with very little feeling of respect by anyone, except perhaps his mother.

The time came in due course when the college of Fort William was reformed. Writers' Buildings were closed as a residential college. The young writers on arriving in India were ordered to remain in Calcutta to obtain a certain qualification in the native languages, but they were expected to live with friends who would keep them under greater social restraint; or to find their own habitations, where it is needless to say that there was no social restraint. The result was that three or four young men who had been friends at the college of Haileybury, in England, joined one another in setting up a house or mess in Calcutta. The Government no longer offered its loan of £400 to each young man. The chief evidence of college discipline (the name of the college being still maintained) consisted in the daily appearance of a venerable native gentleman called a Moonshee or a Pundit; and in a monthly examination in the College Hall, before the Principal and two paid examiners. The venerable native gentlemen who came as instructors in the languages were usually ignorant of English, and were therefore unacceptable to their pupils. They had no personal interest in their pupils, as they drew their Government salary without reference to the progress of their pupils. They attended solemnly from day to day, and were as solemnly requested to come again to-morrow. When a young writer really wished to learn the languages, he invoked the help of one of the two private teachers, Raj Chunder and Harry Mohun who were good English scholars, and so made the path of learning a little more pleasant. Each young writer was required to qualify in the languages in either one or two years after his arrival in India, and so the time came at last when he was obliged to call in the private tutors. Somehow or other these private tutors had a great prophetic power of anticipating the particular passages in the text-books, and the particular papers for translation which would be used at any coming examination. Or if it turned out that they had been mistaken when the day of examination came, they were usually in attendance within reach of the examination hall, and mysteriously entered into some electro-biological or theosophical communication with their pupils, if any of these were nervous or doubtful of their own powers. We would beg, however, emphatically to record that most of the men passed their examinations by their own knowledge and ability. There were always a certain number of men who attained honours and pecuniary rewards and medals for their superior proficiency in the languages; but there were sometimes a few whose idleness and negligence compelled them at the last moment to have recourse to electro-biological assistance.

But whilst the studious existence of the College was thus carried on, its social existence was much more pleasant and influential. Three or four young men living together kept up an establishment which seldom cost any one of them less than £100 per month, his pay from Government being £35. Almost every young civilian used to keep at least three horses and a buggy. The number of their native servants was so large that we hesitate to write it. The use of the hookah was fashionable, and almost every young man kept a man and a boy to look after this elaborate smoking apparatus. Each student had two or three table servants, arrayed in gay liveries with silver crests. Every student belonged to the Bengal Club, to the Racket Club, to the Cricket Club, to the Swimming Club, to the Turf Club, and a few really good riders were admitted to the Tent Club. Proficiency at billiards was a common accomplishment. Play rather than proficiency at whist was the rule, and the stakes were not less than four sovereigns on each rubber, whilst a little quiet betting easily doubled and quadrupled these petty stakes. But there were many other pleasant and necessary expenses. Private parties to ladies, theatricals, and public balls were to be got up at the expense of the young civilians in college, of course in return for the pleasant and ample hospitality extended to them by the residents of Calcutta. Even the expense of dress was not inconsiderable. The usual number of young civilians belonging to the college was about thirty, and at least twenty of this number would appear on the Course, or Rotten Row of Calcutta, every evening, dressed in the highest light of fashion, as an example to the rest of the fashionable world who had been longer exiled from England. But in addition to the ordinary civil society of Calcutta, the young civilian had to keep himself on good terms with the messes of the regiments in Fort

William and at Barrackpore, and at the famous old Artillery mess at Dumdum which was then in its palmy days. It was nothing unusual for a young civilian to entertain a large party of his young friends at the Bengal Club, when champagne flowed like water; sometimes, perhaps, it flowed too freely. There is an old but true story of a young civilian who had been entertaining his friends at the Bengal Club. After dinner, and, we may add, after midnight, he was driving home to his house with his new buggy and his best horse and harness, all purchased within the last week, when at an awkward turn of the road he pulled the wrong rein, and his spirited horse plunged headlong into a deep tank or reservoir of water. How the master and his groom saved their lives is hardly known. The unfortunate horse was drowned, and the buggy was fished out next day looking anything but gay. The young man wrote home to his father, asking for funds to buy a new horse and buggy, but he received a stern reply :—"I cannot understand, my dear son, how a young man in your position can require to keep three horses, three grooms, and a cabriolet." But the good old man sent the money asked for.

At the present day the college of Fort William no longer exists as a college for young civilians. They are so fully crammed and instructed and examined under the competition system that they are supposed to arrive in India fully acquainted with the native languages. They are, therefore, at once sent off to join their official appointments as subordinates in various districts. They have thus no longer any opportunity of exercising or learning to exercise in the capital that social influence which their predecessors enjoyed. Perhaps it is fortunate for society that it is not subjected to the combined and overwhelming galaxy of talent that would be found in a band of twenty or thirty young men radiant with all the honour and glory of successful competition in England, and having as yet had little or no opportunity of finding their proper level with the rest of the working world. We have heard of a story of a young competitive civilian who was asked to dine at the Bengal Club, an institution of which the members are chiefly barristers, merchants, and bankers, with a sprinkling of civilians and military men, who all fancy that they live rather well and generously. "I think," said the young man to his host of the evening, "I could venture to point out to you several solecisms in your club dinner; for instance, the servants actually handed me two kinds of fish at the same time." The host kindly explained that the servants had *shown* the two dishes to the young stranger because he could not understand what they tried to say to him in the native language. Presently, on adjourning to the billiard-room, this young stranger observed an indifferent player pocket his adversary's ball. "Ah," he said, "do you allow that play here? The club to which I belonged in

London considered it ungentlemanly." But, fortunately, competitive civilians of this highly aristocratic breed and exquisite sweetness and light are rather uncommon, and many of them are as fine specimens of manly and well-educated Englishmen as it could be possible to find in any part of the world.

When a young civilian enters upon the active duties of his profession he is first styled an assistant. Under this description he is the assistant to the magistrate and collector of a particular district. He is vested with certain limited judicial and fiscal authority. He can inflict a small amount of imprisonment, and impose moderate fines in the criminal cases which he tries as assistant magistrate. He may be put in charge of the treasury, and have to deal with sundry matters connected with the land revenue in his capacity of assistant collector. The making or marring of a young assistant sometimes depends not a little on the character of the magistrate-collector under whom he is appointed to serve. The assistant may know a great many things, but when he comes face to face with his actual work in office he finds that he has still very much to learn. He is probably stuffed full of English, Mahomedan, and Hindoo law; he has doubtless passed his examinations in the Oriental languages; but when he takes his seat in court he promptly finds that there is something very wrong. The natives by whom he is surrounded apparently do not understand their own language; they pronounce it so strangely that what they say is not intelligible to him. They certainly fail to understand what he says to them; and as to the legal knowledge with which he expected to astonish them, he finds no opportunity for displaying it. He hears something about an Act—and about duffers—and he suspects that he is being rudely chaffed as a duffer. Now-a-days, relief comes to him usually from one of the native officials in attendance on him, who can speak English, and insinuatingly becomes his interpreter—in fact, his guide, philosopher, and friend. But an assistant is often and ought always to be saved from this abrupt and false position, in entering on his duties, if he will take a little quiet instruction from the magistrate and collector under whom he is to serve. When he joins his district he should first practise anatomy on a few defunct bodies, instead of beginning with vivisection on an actual case. If he will read through the records of a few old decided cases, under the friendly guidance of his magistrate, and in the privacy of his own room, he will soon become master of all the leading technicalities and phraseology of the cases which he will ordinarily have to decide. He will soon become used to the language of the native officers appointed to attend on him, and will learn to practise his own tongue to the colloquial abbreviations and expressions which differ so widely from the language of the vernacular text-books. Above all things, let him not fear to ask for an explanation of whatever he does not understand, and let him take a note of the explanation given. In after days he will look back at his notes with much satisfaction and amusement at his own quondam ignorance, and he will be the more ready to give help and instruction to the young men who come after him.

If the assistant will open his eyes and look round him thoughtfully, he will soon come to observe the gravity and importance of the official position which he now holds. The district contains more than a million inhabitants. The assistant will be surprised to find that he holds the fourth place in the official hierarchy of the district. There are the judge, the collector-magistrate, and the joint-magistrate ranking above him, but his official place is fourth on the list. What a difference this is from his position in his native land, where he was probably next to nobody, and certainly exercised no sort of authority. Now he has become the fourth in rank amongst a million of people. Many young men are rather slow to perceive this. Very probably a becoming sense of modesty restrains them from attempting to assert the position. But the fact remains, and the official responsibility positively exists. Many an assistant, owing to the casual illness or temporary absence of his official superiors, has suddenly found himself actually the first official among a million of people. In no other part of the world, in no other condition of society, does official responsibility so suddenly thrust itself on a young man about twenty years of age.

In the ordinary routine of social life at a small civil station, the assistant at first holds a comparatively humble position. A civil station is the capital of a district. The society consists principally of members of the Civil Service; there is the judge, who is usually between thirty and forty years of age; the collector-magistrate is now sometimes senior, sometimes junior, to the judge; next comes the joint-magistrate and deputy-collector, a sort of second in command to the collector-magistrate; and next comes the assistant. Outside this nucleus of the Civil Service there come the police officers, the doctor, the clergyman, and one or two other minor English officials, and perhaps a few independent men employed in mercantile business or owning landed estates. If there is a railway running through the district, it may contribute an engineer to the little society, or there may be an officer of the Public Works Department located there. In Bengal, military detachments very seldom help to swell the numbers of a civil station. In fact, with the ladies of the several families, a party of twenty can seldom be assembled, except on the most important festive occasions.

In a very small world such as this, it is not surprising that the assistant, to some extent, acquiesces in his native designation as the "chota saheb," or little saheb, of the community. He is treated as a new-comer, willing to learn and to be pleased at acquiring experience from the older folks around him. If he is a sensible man, he really feels how very much of practical life he has yet to learn.

After an assistant has been about a year at a district station, and when he has passed certain examinations with which the Government still persists in unnecessarily tormenting its junior servants, he is usually sent to what is called a sub-division of the district. The inventor of sub-divisions was undoubtedly an enemy to his brethren. To be in charge of a sub-division means, in most cases, that the assistant is cut off from all communication with his fellow-Englishmen. He is undoubtedly monarch of all he surveys, but his realms are rather pitiful. He has an official dwelling, usually much out of repair; sometimes it is only a mat and thatched building, but too frequently one part of the building serves as a dwelling-house, and the other part serves as the public office, so that privacy or quiet is almost unattainable. Within a few yards of the dwelling-house the lock-up of the prisoners under trial or under sentence presents itself, with a guard-house for the police detachment. A small tank or pond, in which the prisoners and their guard bathe, also serves to supply the assistant and his domestics with water. There may be some half-cultivated scrap of garden, and sometimes there is actually a bit of road along which a wheeled vehicle can be driven, at least as far as the broken bridge, for the repair of which the estimates have been several months under consideration before some superior officer. The reader may imagine the feelings of the young official on finding himself in charge of such a kingdom as this. There is not another white face to be seen. If he falls ill, there is a half-trained native doctor to attend to him. His nearest white neighbour is probably an indigo-planter, with whom he may not be on good terms, as he may have decided cases adversely to the planter's interests. Meanwhile his official duties are not only onerous but irksome. He is expected to be a jack-of-all-trades. He has complicated criminal cases before him in his magisterial capacity. The native lawyers who practise in his court are usually men of inferior quality, who have not succeeded in their business at the chief station of the district. The native officers who belong to his court are ill-paid, and too often inefficient. They have at the best a very limited experience, and are not qualified to supply the assistant's own want of experience. He has to look after his treasury, and to send in all sorts of accounts to the head-quarters of the district. There is hardly a sub-division in which the accounts are kept correctly. In too many there are embezzlements or some fraudulent practices which the assistant fails to detect until he has become in a measure responsible for them, so that when he discovers them he has practically to report evil of himself. His work is carried on for many hours in a crowded room, in a hot and reeking atmosphere. Just as he hopes that his daily labours are coming to an end, there arrives from a remote police-station a corpse and a confessing murderer. The corpse has to be sent to the native doctor for a post-mortem examination, with such information as the assistant can obtain from the police reports as to the nature of the injuries which caused death. This must be done promptly—for corpses will not keep, in fact, they are often very unpleasant when they reach the assistant's office. Nor will the murderer's confession keep; it must be taken down at once, while the criminal is still in a state of awe and repentance, and faint with hunger. The police are careful not to let a confessing criminal have too much to eat until he has repeated his confession, voluntarily and entirely of his own free will, before the assistant. So, however weary the assistant may be, he must solemnly admonish the prisoner not to confess unless he likes to do so, and then record what the unfortunate creature has to state. When this is over, he hopes to get away, but there is an emergent application for postage-stamps which he does not dare postpone, and he has to count them out from the chest in his little murky den of a treasury, and check all the entries in the account-books before he can close them with a correct balance of the stamps still in store. At last he may gain the privacy of his own rooms, and the company of his sole and faithful companion, his dog. But even then his troubles are not always at an end. Perhaps an alarm of fire is given from the neighbouring village. The sky is red with flames, and dense clouds of smoke fill the air. The assistant quickly mounts his horse, and dashes off to the scene, to try and control the crowd, and to direct the efforts of those few who seem to have their senses left, in attempting to extinguish the flames, or prevent the conflagration from spreading. He will be lucky if he succeeds in doing any good. He will be very lucky if he escapes without some personal injury, and he will probably meet with execrations instead of thanks from those people whose huts have had to be pulled down in order to prevent the fire from spreading.

There is sometimes at a sub-division a great opportunity for getting good sport if the assistant is fond of hunting or shooting. Near the principal station of many districts the game is becoming exhausted; but in a remote sub-division there are usually some natural game-preserves which have not been so often invaded by the adventurous English sportsman. As to snipe, he will probably find them in his own garden any time between September and March; and the rice-swamps which come up to the edge of his garden are sure to be full of snipe in different places as the waters of the annual inundation begin to subside. Wild ducks of infinite variety and in numbers innumerable are to be found in some of the quiet inland backwaters branching from the nearest great river. The wild hogs are seldom wanting. The villagers will gladly point out these dangerous enemies to their crops; and if the ground is rideable, some friends with their horses and spears may occasionally be brought together for a good day's sport. Leopards are to be heard of in many villages, and when a particular leopard makes itself troublesome by killing the goats of the villagers or perhaps scratching and wounding some old woman, the assistant will be asked to go and shoot it. Tigers are scarce animals now; but they roam over large distances, and a tiger sometimes makes its appearance and establishes itself in a village, to the utter dismay of the inhabitants, who see their cattle killed daily, and live in constant apprehension for their own safety. But when a tiger is thus heard of, let the assistant not trust too much to his own prowess, or to the aid of any native companions who are willing to accompany him to kill the tiger. Let him remember the fate of poor Langdon, who went out a few years ago with a single-barrelled gun in his hand and a revolver in his belt to slay a tiger that had taken up its abode in a neighbouring village. He was attended by a crowd of natives armed with matchlocks, swords, and clubs. They formed a sort of line and advanced upon the tiger, who was sitting on his haunches in an open rice-field, looking at them. Poor Langdon fired his single barrel when he was about twenty yards from the tiger. He probably missed the beast, who came down with a bound and seized him by the neck and killed him like a terrier kills a rat. His native companions very naturally took to their heels. They are hardly to be blamed. They had little chance of killing the tiger, and their only safety was in flight. Not long previous to poor Langdon's death a stray tiger similarly visited another district, and two or three of the young civilians, with a police officer who had shot many tigers, made an expedition to slay it. They found the tiger lying by a little hut in an open field. They approached cautiously, and made certain of their prey. A crowd of gaping villagers watched them from a high bank of earth, which seemed a safe place of refuge. At a given signal the experienced police-officer fired the first shot, and his companions each fired off both barrels. The tiger rose unharmed and looked at them; but fortunately his wrath was directed to the noisy native villagers on the high bank and he rushed off towards them, scattering them like a flock of sheep. The young officials and their police-mentor returned to their homes sadder and wiser men, not likely to go out again on foot in quest of a tiger.

The life of an assistant civilian at a sub-division is a life of toil and drudgery. But relief may come unexpectedly. One gloomy day, when his misfortunes seem at their worst, he finds a letter informing him that he has been appointed to act as under-secretary to the Government of the province. He can hardly understand or believe, at first, the good fortune that has come to him. He had begun to fancy that he was forgotten by all the world and by his friends. But when he tells the news to his native officials they are not slow to congratulate him. They tell him how under-secretaries are the men who eventually become lieutenant-governors. They almost worship him, and pray that their humble services may not be forgotten when he comes into his kingdom. But he must wait anxiously for a few days until his successor comes to relieve him, and then he rushes off eagerly to the capital, with hardly less change in his position and prospects than that of the butterfly who has emerged from his previous humble form.

In the ordinary routine of the career of an Indian civilian in Bengal, he rises from an assistant to be a joint-magistrate, and he then becomes either a collector-magistrate or a judge of a district—and he never emerges from this quiet and hard-working career. If he is a judge he may, after twenty years or more, hope to obtain a seat in the High Court. If he is a collector-magistrate he may similarly hope to become a commissioner, and eventually to rise to be a member of the Board of Revenue. But outside the ordinary routine of appointments there are a certain number of offices which may be considered to be the special prizes of the service. To get into the secretariat is the very laudable desire of almost every young civilian. In the first place the pay of the under-secretary is very much larger than that of most of his contemporaries. But the pay is mere dross in comparison with the power and change of position which a secretariat appointment confers. His other brethren are the ordinary rank and file—but he has become an officer in command, and he issues his orders accordingly. It is much more pleasant to command than to obey, especially to those who have themselves been disciplined in the school of obedience. It is true that the under-secretary, in writing an official letter, informs his correspondent that he is directed by his honour the lieutenant-governor of the province to bid him do this or abstain from doing that; but the personality of the under-secretary is not always concealed, or rather it derives part of its glory and brilliancy from the association of his name with that of the lieutenant-governor. But it is not merely to his own friends and contemporaries that the young under-secretary stands forth as the representative of the highest authority. When he was an assistant he may have demeaned himself humbly before the collector-magistrate who was his immediate master. He probably felt a sort of mysterious awe as regards the officer styled a commissioner of division, who is the superior master of several collector-magistrates and their assistants. But as an under-secretary he finds himself issuing orders to these commissioners, with instructions to them to communicate his orders to the collector-magistrates. In fact, official etiquette in the secretariat almost precludes him from direct communication with his former superior, the collector-magistrate. There is yet another strong point of contrast between the position of the under-secretary and that of his unpromoted brethren, the sub-divisional officers whom we have tried to describe. The latter have hardly anyone to help them in their offices. Their work is usually carried on in a noisy, crowded room, with many interruptions. They have to draft their own letters, and will do wisely even to examine the despatch copies made by their clerks. But in the secretariat everything is very different. The under-secretary has his comfortable and quiet room, to which no one has access except on business, and with his permission. His work is all neatly prepared for him. The red-taped bundles are sorted in their proper boxes. Office-notes are put up explaining the subject, or giving a convenient clue to important papers. If anything appears obscure the under-secretary touches his bell and summons an experienced office-clerk to his aid. He can order further information to be supplied from the office. But, above all, he finds a draft, put up from the office, of almost every letter that is to issue. It is much less laborious work to sign a well-prepared draft, or even to correct an ill-composed draft, than to have to write each letter with his own hand. When the despatch copies of the letters are brought for his signature he signs them by the dozen bravely, and trusts to the office "examiner" for their correctness. There are, of course, many important cases where the under-secretary must compile notes, and prepare the papers for submission to his superior, the secretary, and he must expect sometimes to have them sent back to him from the secretary for further elucidation. Sometimes the secretary or the lieutenant-governor himself wants some orders issued very urgently, and the under-secretary may have a few hours of hard work, or slavery, if he likes to call it so. But, as a rule, he has a very pleasant time of it in his office; and if he keeps his work well in hand, and does not allow any arrears of bundles to accumulate against him, he will discover the value of the motto "*Mihi res non me rebus*," and will find little to interfere with his enjoyment of the social pleasures of the capital. He may even find time for hunting and shooting, if such are his tastes. He can ride and play polo, or he can make his choice between rackets and lawn-tennis, or cricket when cricket is in season. The doors of every fashionable house are open to him if he chooses to leave his card. If he is a good musician he will be all the more welcome. If he can dance well he will have no difficulty in finding partners. At his club he becomes a sort of authority, and has to practice the affectation of being mysterious about trifles, so as to keep himself in training to baffle inconvenient questions on official matters of importance. Whatever social pleasures and amenities life in the capital of Bengal affords, these are all at the disposal of the fortunate civilian under-secretary.

We have hitherto written of the junior officers in the Civil Service. Promotion in the ordinary course is regulated principally by seniority. The whole scheme of the Civil Service in Bengal and in the other provinces of India is like the iron frame-work of a machine, in which all the principal parts consist of members of the Civil Service. As the older members are used up and worn out, the younger members are fitted into their places. The Government sometimes removes a man who does not seem strong enough for his share in the work, and transfers him to a position where the strain on his power is less, and replaces him by a stronger man. To most men the first direct object of their ambition is to obtain charge of a district. After about ten years of subordinate service, the civilian finds himself appointed as collector and magistrate to the charge of a district, and he thus becomes the direct representative of the executive government of the country. The title "collector-magistrate" is somewhat vague and misleading, especially to English readers unacquainted with India. The word "collector" has no special dignity or authority about it. Our own juvenile reminiscence of a collector in England was of the local collector of taxes, a man with a white apron and a pen behind his ear, and a portable ink-bottle at his waist. An Indian collector, at least in Bengal, is a collector almost only in name. The revenues of the district are doubtless collected under his superintendence, but he has almost as little connection personally with the actual collection as the Governor of the Bank of England has with the sovereigns and bank-notes which pass through his bank. The title of "magistrate" is scarcely less misleading.

It is true that he is the chief magistrate of the district, but he has very little direct concern with the actual trial of the criminal cases in his district. But the title of "collector-magistrate" exists in Bengal, and therefore we must deal with it. In reality he is the administrator of a small province which contains a population from one to two million inhabitants. For the details of his administration he has civilian and non-civilian subordinates, each of whom is invested with certain fiscal or magisterial powers. He distributes the work of the district amongst these officers. To one he assigns the care of his treasury and accounts; to another he delegates the management of the excise; to a third he makes over the duty of measuring and assessing landed estates which require a readjustment of the burden of their land revenue; to a fourth he entrusts the special care of those properties belonging to minors and others which come under him as the representative of the Court of Wards. In his magisterial capacity he makes over certain classes of criminal cases to certain subordinates, or assigns to them a limited local jurisdiction for the criminal cases that may occur in it. He is the head of the police of the district, although he has a special officer styled the district superintendent of police by whom all the details of police work are carried on. He is usually the chairman of municipal committees, and of any local body of management connected with education, hospitals, or charitable dispensaries. All schools, especially vernacular schools, are supposed to be his peculiar care. The local jail and its prisoners are under his control, though the doctor or some special officer is in immediate charge of the jail. He is expected to keep himself well-informed as to the trading and commercial interests of the district, and is responsible for the care of the roads and bridges throughout the country. He is expected to keep himself well-informed of all that is going on in the subdivisions of his district which are in the immediate charge of the sub-divisional officers whom we have already described. If cattle-disease breaks out in the interior, he is expected to report on it and take measures to put an end to it. If fever or cholera begin to devastate any part of his dominion, he must at once take action to contend with the enemy. If troops are marching through the district, he must see to the clearance of the encampment grounds, and to the provision of rations for the soldiers and their camp-followers. If there is no clergyman at the station, he may be called on to baptise infant children, and much more certainly to bury anyone who dies. He will have also to provide for the conduct of the weekly church service. We have by no means exhausted the list of his duties; but finally, if a prisoner in his jurisdiction is sentenced to be hung, it will be his duty to superintend the execution. He is held personally responsible by the Government that everything goes right in the district. He has many hands to help him in the details of his numerous duties, but still he is expected to put his own finger occasionally into every man's pie; and if he abstains as much as possible from exercising any primary authority, there is hardly a matter in which he is not referred to as the appellate authority by those who are dissatisfied with the orders of his subordinates. To carry out all his functions he should be an Argus and a Briareus. He is often a little sickly-looking man in spectacles.

CHAPTER V.

THE BENGAL CIVIL SERVICE (*continued*).

THOSE who have seen Tom Taylor's play, "The Overland Route" at the Haymarket Theatre, have probably been amused at the representation of the old civilians Sir Solomon Fraser, K.C.B., and Mr. Colepepper, who are two of the principal characters of the piece. It may also be said to afford a favourable opportunity for old Indians of seeing themselves as others see them. Sir Solomon is the representative of the old school of political officers, who passed the chief part of their life as residents in native independent states. Mr. Colepepper is the hard-working old man who finished his career in the service as a commissioner, without any special rewards or titles, and under some mysterious liability to Government for many thousands of pounds, certain vouchers having been lost in the mutinies. With reference to these imaginary individuals we will give a brief sketch of a few more of the many branches into which the career of an Indian civilian may develop itself.

The Political Department, as it was called, in India, was for a long time considered the most eligible and enviable line in which a young civil officer could shape his career. There was a time when the most promising young men were specially selected by Government, and sent off to the famous capital at Hyderabad to graduate under the guidance of the eminent chief Charles Metcalfe, then resident at that native court. Residents and Governor-General's agents were formerly to be found in many parts of India. The resident was the officer who was supposed to advise, or, we ought to say, imperceptibly to influence, the independent native prince or princess to whose court he was accredited. The Governor-General's agent was the representative of British authority, or, to put it more plainly, the instructor or bear-leader of those native princes whose authority was not independent, but who needed to be instructed or to be led according to their own individual capacity or incapacity in exercising their own limited power and jurisdiction. The officer employed in either position was supposed to be well-versed in all matters connected with the etiquette and ceremonial of native courts, and it was essential that he himself should be distinguished for his grave and imperturbable courtesy of demeanour and speech. He was expected to be a master of all the arts of intrigue, not so much for the purpose of carrying on any active intrigue, but rather for the sake of baffling those intrigues which are the life and breath of a native court, where mine must occasionally be met by counter-mine. For the word intrigue includes, and indeed usually consists of, the very smallest matters, in dealing with which the political officer only keeps his weapons sharpened in readiness to deal with any matter of real gravity and importance. A resident formerly was almost isolated from the fellowship of his own countrymen, save of those who constituted his own staff or assistants. But this form of society is always mentally unwholesome, as the chief finds no one who is prepared openly to differ from his opinions, or to maintain any serious argument against him. Hence the resident of the pre-mutiny period sometimes became a rather pompous self-opiniated punctilious and artificial sort of person, who is exemplified in Sir Solomon Fraser, K.C.B. The race of political officers is now comparatively extinct, and the circumstances under which they exist have been so materially altered by the introduction of railways and the general improvement in the means of interchanging ideas with their fellow-men, that any man who allowed himself to acquire the ways and habits of his fossil predecessors would probably be deemed unfit for his post, although he will still be careful to observe the professional courtesy and demeanour for which we ought not to fail to give due credit to the members of the old school of politicals. Writing as we are with reference to the province of Bengal, it may be said that political residents are non-existent, and the few Governor-General's agents, who are still employed at the Court of the Nawab of Morshedabad and on some of the frontier divisions, have been much shorn of their honours and emoluments.

With regard to Mr. Colepepper, who has been presented in the play as the type of the commissioner, we do not mean to say that the portrait will be actually recognised, as there are few now left who are able to identify the men who served their country so well and so patiently both before and during the mutinies; but we are inclined to think that someone has unconsciously sat for his portrait on this occasion, and we do not feel that he has anything to be ashamed of in it. A man who has spent his life under an Eastern sun, surrounded by Oriental influences, must not suppose that he is like his contemporaries who have never left the shores of England. His curious garb, his white sun-hat, his thin white coat and trousers, present as great a contrast to the broad-cloth garments and regulation hat of his English compeer as may be found in their respective thoughts and feelings. And we are not at all prepared to admit that all the mental advantage or even the physical superiority is on the side of the stay-at-home Englishman. It may be that the man who has served in India has attained all his Oriental learning and practical administrative experience in addition to his natural privileges and mental acquirements as an Englishman. He has, perhaps, seen some things from the wrong end of the telescope; but have his brethren in England always taken a more correct view of Indian objects? The heart and mind of the one have probably been enlarged by an enlightened sympathy for millions of new and strange people, whilst the other has passed his life in the narrow prejudices of his own profession or business, and in the surroundings of his own country parish. The one may have endured the burden and heat of the sun, which has blanched the colour from his cheeks, and left him a lean and yellow visage and disorganised liver. But is the other very much better off who has grown corpulent and unwieldy with too much good-living and too much old port wine, whilst his limbs are often racked by rheumatism, if he has not become a victim to gout and dyspepsia?

However, though there may be individual exceptions to every rule, the mind of the British public is tolerably well made up that Mr. Colepepper is a genuine specimen commissioner of the Indian Civil Service, and we are content to leave them in that belief. But the title of commissioner conveys no sort of distinct idea to the English mind. It is curious how wanting many Indian titles are in precision, or even in affording any suggestion of their meaning. We remember a story where a good-natured old commissioner was sitting at dinner next the colonel of a regiment which had just come to Calcutta from the North-West Provinces. The commissioner casually said to the colonel, "I am the animal which is called a commissioner in this part of the world." The colonel was immensely delighted. He had been accustomed to their high mightinesses the commissioners of the North-West Provinces; and it was a strange thing to him to find a commissioner speaking almost disrespectfully of his own title. But there are commissioners and commissioners. The commissioner in Bengal is the officer in chief executive charge of a territorial division, each division containing six or seven separate districts, with a total population of about eight or ten millions inhabitants. There are some divisions in which for geographical reasons the area is smaller, and the population of the division less numerous. The commissioner is usually an officer in what may be called the prime of Indian official life, about forty years of age, and of about twenty years' standing in his service. He is usually selected by Government from the executive officers known as collector-magistrates of districts, and the selection not unfrequently causes considerable jealousy and dissatisfaction, especially if the selected commissioner happens to be junior to any of the collector-magistrates in the division to which he is appointed. The commissioner is the local representative of Government in his own division. The Government sends its orders to him, and he passes them on to the collector-magistrates.

On the same principle the collector-magistrates submit their reports to Government through the commissioner. He is the chief local authority, save that the district judges are entirely independent of him; and the judicial independent authority thus established is the recognised constitutional safety-valve, which is intended to provide against any injudicious or casual stretch of authority on the part of the executive. The commissioner is the head of the police throughout his division; but here again there are some subtle niceties of discipline and practice. The commissioner receives written reports from the police, through the district-magistrate, of the progress of their investigations in all heinous and important cases. But his power is limited. He cannot issue direct orders to the actual police-officers investigating a case, so as to bid them arrest one suspected person or release another. He may offer friendly advice and suggestions to the magistrate with regard to the action of the police; and he may also, if dissatisfied with their proceedings, make unpleasant remarks and comments. But the discipline of the police force is regulated by a hierarchy of its own, consisting of district-superintendents and deputy inspectors-general, and an inspector-general, who is equal in official rank to the commissioner, and in direct communication with Government. And as the commissioner may interfere with the police only under certain limitations, so, on the other hand, he must be very cautious to abstain from interference with any case the moment that it has been sent up by the police for trial before any magisterial or judicial officer. Any interference by the executive in the judicial trial of a case is strongly resented; but it is open to a commissioner to set the public prosecutor in motion, or to employ special counsel to look after the effective prosecution of a difficult and important case. Eventually, if a particular case, or any class of cases, becomes of such deep interest as to require the attention of Government—or if the Government has called for a report—it is the commissioner who has to represent the whole of the facts to Government, and it is then open to him to express his opinion unreservedly on the good or bad conduct of the police, and this is also his opportunity for pointing out to Government any defects that may have occurred in the judicial proceedings. But in this part of the business he will do well to temper his words with discretion. If the commissioner expresses an opinion, in his report to Government, that the magistrate or judge who tried the case has made any serious mistake as to his facts or to his law, this practically amounts to a proclamation of war. The Government on receiving the commissioner's report to this effect will not be in a hurry to pronounce an opinion. It will probably send the report of the commissioner to the judges of the High Court, and will request them to inquire and report what the magistrate or judge has to say on his own behalf. Of course the magistrate or judge in most instances stoutly maintains that he was right, and it may be that the judges of the

High Court also take the part of the judge or magistrate, or at all events extenuate his errors. Then the Government may either give the commissioner an opportunity for a rejoinder, or it may proceed to put an end to the case by passing a decision on it. The approved Government secretariat style of decision is to find a little fault with everybody; and the principle of decisions of this kind is simple and obvious, because it discourages all the officers concerned from desiring again to bring their quarrels or differences into prominence, so that they will not come up bothering the Government again for a long time to come. It may be observed that the Government is usually very careful to agree as far as possible with the judges of the High Court, and to throw over the complainant commissioner. So the commissioner probably finds, to his annoyance, that he has taken a great deal of trouble to do his duty, with the highly satisfactory result that he is told, like a naughty boy, not to do it again.

The commissioner is also the chief revenue authority throughout his division, the collectors being his subordinates in this capacity, whilst he himself is directly subject to the control of the Board of Revenue. In most parts of Bengal, the collection of the ordinary Land Revenue gives no trouble. The instalments of the Government Revenue are paid in with a punctuality which would gratify any Government under the sun. This is one of the fortunate results of the much-abused permanent settlement in Bengal, the very mention of which is so like a red rag to a bull with some persons, that we shall say no more about it, except to observe that there are some other well-informed persons who believe that if there had been no permanent settlement in Bengal in 1793, there would have been no British authority left in India in 1883. According to the true British method of procedure, the Government being now fully secure in its own share of the Land Revenue from the land-owners, has so altered and modified the laws which it made for the protection of the land-owners in the collection of their rents that it leaves them to collect them as best they may. The latest device is to compel the land-owner to sue his defaulting tenants in the civil courts, as they are pleasantly called, so that the Government derives a large indirect revenue through its stamp laws, an *ad valorem* stamp being required on the institution of a suit; whilst the costs of the case are a heavy addition to the tenant's rent if the suit is decided against him, as it must almost always be decided from the nature of things. But this is all the result of pure benevolence and the well-meaning but possibly misguided kindness of those philanthropists who have constituted themselves the champions of the poor tenant, with no very complete understanding of the poor tenant's real wants and necessities. Be this as it may, the commissioner and the collector have now very little trouble in the collection of the Government land revenue in Bengal.

Occasionally a landed estate, as it is officially called, is sold by auction for non-payment of revenue; and if the owner of the defaulting estate is dissatisfied, he appeals to the commissioner to quash the auction sale. But it is very seldom that an estate is sold at auction, except with the wish and knowledge of the owners. An auction-sale conveys a clear and indefeasible title on the purchaser, who can thus afford to pay a much higher price for the property than if he attempted to buy it privately, for where there are many shareholders in an estate it almost passes the skill of the most able legal conveyancer to devise a perfect title exhaustive of all previously existing rights and encumbrances. With regard to the other revenue duties of a commissioner, they are more easily enumerated than they can be described or made intelligible. He has to provide for the management of the estates of minors, lunatics, and others, which have come under the control of the Court of Wards. He has to keep an eye on the great gains or losses arising from alluvion and diluvion along the banks of the huge rivers which sweep through Bengal, changing their courses and washing away their banks, not merely by a few yards, but sometimes by miles at a time. The commissioner has to look after the excise revenue of the districts under him. He must take thought regarding the application of the stamp laws, and be prepared to explain to the Board of Revenue the reason why the stamp revenue increases in one district and decreases in another district. This is sometimes a rather difficult task, as the collector in whose district an increase is shown blandly attributes it to the abundance of the harvest; whilst, unfortunately, the collector of the district in which a decrease appears also attributes the decrease to the abundance of the harvest; and though it is perfectly possible that there may be some truth in each of these explanations, it will not do for the commissioner to send up both explanations to the Board in their conflicting nudity and crudity. The commissioner has also to superintend the collection of that very curious tax which is known under the name of the license-tax. It is the only existing form of direct personal taxation, and is apparently called the license-tax because the Government was not permitted to call it an income-tax. A previous Government had taken much credit to itself for the abolition of the income-tax, and neither political party in England is now willing to allow itself to be connected with the re-imposition of the income-tax. But as some sort of direct taxation was deemed necessary, and is admittedly necessary, in order to reach the rich trading classes, it was introduced under the name of a license-tax, whilst it is only a disguised and deformed income-tax, utterly failing to produce the amount which would be derived from a well-administered income-tax, and only tolerated because the taxpayers subject to it are well aware that almost any change in the law is likely to add to the amount of their taxation. The original income-tax was abolished when it had begun to work, quite smoothly, in Lower Bengal, and the chief defects of the law had been eradicated and cured. Its ghost, the license-tax, now reigns in its stead, and people who pay the license-tax receive a license to do nothing, or, in some cases, to carry on the business for which they have to pay another license-tax under the local municipal laws.

The commissioner of a division has his head-quarters at one of the principal stations of the districts subject to his authority; but he is expected to make at least one tour of inspection in the course of the year, so as to visit all his districts. In some divisions the railways now make travelling easy, and his visitations can be made at any time that suits his convenience. But there are some divisions in which there are no railways, and even the local roads are hardly passable except at certain times of the year. In some parts the broad rivers afford the only means of communication, and he has to travel by boat or steamer. The commissioner's visit of inspection in remote districts is one of the important events of the year. The officials, with their usual hospitality, make every effort to welcome and entertain him. The principal native residents of the district come in from their country residences with a large band of their retainers to pay their respects to him, and to represent their wishes, and also their grievances. He has to inspect the public offices and to satisfy himself in many matters of detail, such, for instance, as the amount of treasure contained in the collector's treasury, and the number of stamps, including postage stamps, which are or ought to be in the collector's custody. He has to visit all the local schools and pose as an amateur examiner in history and mathematics and the vernacular languages. He must inspect the local jail and lunatic asylum; not interfering in their management, as they are under special dèpartments, but recording in the visitor's book his opinion on what he sees, and on what he conceives to be wanting for the improvement of these establishments. He must inspect the old burial-grounds, and see that due care is taken of the monuments and tombstones of the otherwise long-forgotten dead. The opportunity of his visit will probably be taken to hold a public meeting to encourage subscriptions in support of some local charitable institutions, such as hospitals and dispensaries, or for the construction of some new work of public utility, such as a new road or bridge. And if any local feuds or factions exist, either among the English residents or in different sections of the native community, he is expected to act as a peacemaker, and to devise a *modus vivendi* for the future.

The duties of a commissioner are almost as varied and numerous as it is possible to imagine, but he must also fully appreciate the doctrine lately enunciated by Mr. Gladstone regarding the duties of the Chancellor of the Exchequer. It is not sufficient that he shall deal with all the work that comes to his hand, but he must have time to look about him, and seek for and make work, and initiate those reforms and improvements for which there is such ample opportunity in almost every condition of civilised society. He must be prepared for disappointment as well as encouragement in his endeavours to do good. Sometimes his own subordinates fail to support or adopt his proposals, or a zealous and active subordinate who gladly and eagerly carried out his plans is removed to some other sphere of usefulness, whilst his successor is a man who cares for nothing but his own ideas and abhors all unnecessary responsibility. Sometimes the Government discredits and discountenances his well-meant proposals, and he is graciously informed that local knowledge is always wrong—a curious paradox at first sight, but not by any means devoid of truth when analysed from the broader Government point of view. On the whole, the life and work of a commissioner is, or ought to be, exceedingly enjoyable to a man of active mind and body; but when mental and bodily activity are impaired, it only remains for a commissioner to retire like Mr. Colepepper to his native country to spend the remainder of his days in dignified repose.

There are still several positions in the life of a civilian which may be worthy of more than passing notice. When an officer has elected to join the judicial branch of the service, he in course of time becomes the judge of a district, an officer of much authority and dignity, and not badly remunerated. The position of a judge has one feature in it which makes it highly commendable, especially in contrast with that of the collector-magistrate, who has elected the executive branch. The latter officer has many masters, and his time is never his own, and even his private house is not sacred against the invasions of emergent business. But the judge has but one master, the High Court. He goes to his court at a fixed hour, and leaves it also at the appointed time, and he regulates these hours according to his own convenience. His business is carried on solely in his court; when he leaves his court his work is at an end. It would be considered both unbecoming and irregular for any suitor or pleader to seek to follow him to his own house. The duty of a judge is not so difficult as some people suppose. It is a well-known truism that in almost all law-suits the difficulty is to ascertain the real facts of the case. If the facts are found, the application of the law to those facts is a comparatively simple process. In the court of a district judge there are pleaders of good ability and considerable legal acquirements, who are not likely to allow him to be misled as to the law, however much they may strive to twist the facts of a case in favour of their client. The greater part of a judge's work consists in hearing appeals from the decisions of the native judges subordinate to him, so that he has only to deal with the written evidence on the record, the effect of which has been usually well-weighed and represented in the decision of the subordinate judge. The judge, therefore, can easily master the leading facts of a case as set forth in the decision of the lower court, before he begins to hear the arguments of the counsel who appear to impugn or to support that decision. A case may be more or less complicated, but for a man of ordinary capacity and common sense it is a pleasant intellectual entertainment to listen to the arguments of the contending pleaders. Most of the leading pleaders can speak English well, and state their cases and arguments with a lucidity which might meet with the approval of Matthew Arnold. It only remains for the judge to prepare and pronounce his decision; and if he is a prudent man he will write out his decision in the quiet and privacy of his own study. This is the more necessary because the judge's decision in its turn may become the subject of appeal to the High Court, and it therefore behoves a judge to try to make his decision impregnable.

The most difficult part of a judge's duty consists in trying criminal cases at the sessions. When an accused person is committed by a magistrate on a charge of murder or any other offence with which the magistrate cannot deal finally, he is tried by the sessions judge and by a jury of his countrymen. The prosecution is usually conducted by the Government pleader, whilst the accused retains the services of the best counsel that he can afford to pay. The judge records the evidence in English with his own hand, being himself the interpreter of the actual words in the native language in which it is delivered, whilst simultaneously a native clerk records, or is supposed to record, the actual words spoken by the witness. This imposes a severe task on the judge. He has to listen to what the witness says in the vernacular, he has to interpret and record its meaning in English, and he has to consider the effect of each successive question and answer on the whole of the witnesses' evidence. This triple mental operation is very severe, and imposes too hard a strain upon the judge. When the evidence for the prosecution and the defence is completed, and the counsel on either side have exhausted their eloquence, the judge has the pleasure of summing up the evidence and directing the jury in their vernacular language, a rather arduous task, but we have heard many men do it with much credit to themselves. Perhaps some of our judges in England would not be quite at ease if they had to sum up the evidence and address an English jury in French, or in dog-Latin; but the suggestion may convey to the reader some idea of the difficulty to which an English judge in India is subject. Finally, the judge records his decision elaborately in English, in case the prisoner, if convicted, should appeal to the High Court against his sentence.

From the ranks of the district judges the best men

are selected for a seat in the High Court of Calcutta. It is not very easy to select the best men, and the process of selection is uncertain, because the patronage is exercised nominally by the Viceroy, who has the least actual knowledge of the merits of individual officers, and must therefore be guided by the advice of others. We are prepared to admit that usually the best men are selected, but on every occasion there are several men who consider their own claims superior to those of the officer selected. The position of a judge of the High Court is certainly a very enviable one. It may be said to combine almost the highest amount of official dignity with no inconsiderable degree of otium. In the usual routine of the court work two judges sit together, and constitute what is called a bench. When two judges are sitting together it follows as a matter of course that one of them takes the leading part in the conduct of the case which is before them. Where two men ride on one horse, one must ride behind the other. As a matter of practice, where several cases come before them on the same day, they take the conduct of the cases alternately; but sometimes, where one judge is of a more masterly temperament than the other, he practically assumes the management of every case, whilst the other judge acquiesces in the arrangement. This leads to a powerful development of what has been called the power of the cypher. One judge, Mr. A., is a masterly man, and he scores as 1. The other judge follows his lead, and he therefore scores as 0. But 1 and 0 count ten, and in practice the working power of a bench thus constituted is far more effective than that of a bench where the two judges are antagonistic to one another and are disposed to take conflicting views of a case. It is therefore easy to conceive that whenever a judge is not disinclined to subordinate his own mental powers to those of his colleague, he can pass his time on the bench without any great strain on his intellectual faculties. He may be supposed to be taking copious notes of the arguments, but as a fact he is inditing an overland letter to his absent wife or his children in England. When the case is ripe for decision, and the arguments of counsel are at an end, a brief conference with his colleague satisfies his conscience, and he is prepared to sign his name in concurrence to the decision more or less elaborate which his colleague is ready to compose. The hours during which the High Court sits are not very long or exhausting. The judges usually take their seats at 11 o'clock, and after a sitting of three hours the court withdraws at 2 o'clock for lunch, the contending counsel gladly following their example. It is nearly 3 o'clock before the judges resume their seats on the bench, and by the time that the clock has rolled on to 4, it begins to be a question whether, on the conclusion of a particular case, there is sufficient time to take up and finish a new case, and so it not unfrequently happens that about 4 o'clock the judges retire to their carriages and are driven home to take their rest. At all events, 5 o'clock is the appointed hour for their rising, be the case finished or unfinished; so that it may be taken that about five hours of work is considered a good day's average sitting. Each judge is accustomed to take one day in the week at home for the purpose of writing out his decisions, and for certain administrative and consultative functions. It not unfrequently happens that a judge, on arriving at court, finds that his colleague on the bench is disabled by indisposition from attending court, so that he is obliged to go home again for the day, unless it so chances that another judge on another bench is casually indisposed, and then the two odd men may combine and make up a sort of scratch bench between them for the day.

Whilst the ordinary daily work of a High Court judge is not very severe, the judges are indulged in a much longer vacation, and they have many more holidays than any other class of Government officials. We do not grudge them their holidays, and we are of opinion that many Government officers would be much more competent to work with full mental and bodily vigour if they had a few more holidays and enforced periods of rest. The judges of the High Court have an annual long vacation extending over a period of two months, from about the beginning of September to the beginning of November, when the season, especially in Calcutta, may be said to be most unhealthy and unfavourable to the English constitution. The High Court also closes for a week or ten days at Christmas, and for a similar period at Easter. The native Hindoo and Mahomedan holidays, which come on fixed or variable dates, are religiously observed in the High Court. An eclipse of the sun or moon, if visible, becomes the occasion for a holiday, out of deference to native feeling. We are sorry to say that there is a growing tendency to mutilate and diminish the holiday privileges of the judges. It was formerly open to them to combine a month's privilege leave, under the Service Leave Rules, with the long vacation of the court, so that they got a holiday of three months, which enabled them to pay a flying visit to England. Sundry old gentlemen at the India Office are said to have taken offence at the sight of several High Court judges making their appearance in London for a few days, and actually entitled to their full pay whilst thus absent from duty. This was the real *gravamen* of the offence. It has always been a sort of principle in connection with leave of any kind to mulct the delinquent of his official salary, and so starve him into a return to his duty. It was, therefore, deemed to be an infringement of this principle that a judge should be seen walking about London with his pockets full of rupees, just as if he were in the streets of Calcutta. We are not able to give the precise history of the official communications between the India Office in London and the Government of India at Simla. But it may be easily understood with how much virtuous zeal and good-will the authorities at Simla set themselves to work to give effect to the suggestions of the India Office. The Viceroy and his Councillors, and the secretaries at Simla, are not in the habit of taking any holidays. What are holidays to them when they are living in a cool and healthy climate, drawing salaries which were fixed on a scale suitable to a warmer temperature? Their only avowed relaxation is found in the interval of the moves from Calcutta to Simla, and from Simla back to Calcutta, when their offices are temporarily closed, and their travelling expenses are defrayed by Government. The financial secretary and his department always go to Simla, and they never feel the beam that is in their own eyes, however diligently they espy the motes when an ordinary toiler in the hot plains wants his travelling expenses paid. So it has come to pass that between the parsimony of the India Office, where the scale of salaries is notoriously so low, and the unsympathising sternness of the Indian Government at Simla (sometimes called Capua), the poor judges of the High Court have been shorn of many of their leave privileges; and, even worse, a reduced rate of salary has now been assigned to them. At the end of the last century, we believe, some of the judges of the old Supreme Court went to court in palanqueens, with a stately retinue of sontaburdars, and chobdars, and khidmudgars, and hookahburdars, and chuprassies, and peadahs. Perhaps the time is not remote when we shall see the impoverished High Court judge making his way along Chowringhee Road in a tram-car, and taking a dirty hired palkee to convey him from the nearest point of the tramway to the entrance of the court-house. The leading barristers of the court make an income of £10,000 a year, and will probably give an occasional lift in their carriages to the poor judges who can no longer afford to keep a carriage and horse of their own. Sometimes briefless young barristers may be seen walking early to court, to spend the day in the bar-library, and tramping back again at sunset to their homes. They will hereafter probably find themselves in the honourable company of some of the under-paid judges of their court, who desire to combine exercise with economy.

There is one other position or grade in the Civil Service which we must not omit to describe. A seat in the Board of Revenue is the object of ambition set before commissioners and all executive officers as the reward of their persevering labours and acknowledged merit. Unfortunately it is a haven which few are destined to enter and to be at rest. In the good old days, forty years ago, there were two Boards, each Board consisting of three members. One Board was styled the Board of Land Revenue, the other was the Board of Customs, Salt, and Opium. Each Board had its own separate office and establishment, and its senior and junior civilian secretaries. In those good times there was a chance for many men of arriving at the dignity of a seat in one of the two Boards. But a wicked man was found, whose name must not be even mentioned, who proclaimed to the world that "Boards are screens," and so the days of Boards were numbered, and the screen which for so many long years had served as a cover to the multitudinous sins of Government (yes, of Government, and not of the Board itself) was ruthlessly torn down. The Board consists now only of two members, who are expected to carry on the work for which six men were formerly needed, and their four secretaries have been reduced to two. Nor is this the only change. The Board is now a Board only in name. The two members take charge of separate departments, and each member carries on his work independently, and without consultation with his colleague, except in some few special matters which it is needless to enumerate. One member takes the Land Revenue Department, which provides him with plenty of employment. The other member takes what is absurdly called the Miscellaneous Land Revenue Department, which includes the Excise, Customs, Salt and Opium, Stamps and Stationery, and License-Tax Departments, with a few odds and ends from the Land Revenue (proper), such as the acquisition of land for public purposes, and the partition of landed estates. Occasionally the two members sit together to hear appeals, when there is a probability that the decision of a commissioner will be reversed, as the concurrence of both members is required to set aside the decision of such an experienced officer as a commissioner.

An appeal before the Board is usually supported by the most able counsel in the capital; and where the litigants are wealthy it is not uncommon to see the Advocate-General and two or three of the leading members of the High Court bar arrayed on one side, whilst on the other side the Government Solicitor-General and several other barristers are retained regardless of expense. Some serious dispute regarding land has arisen, and though the intrinsic value of the *causa belli* may be but small, it is a point of honour which neither side can yield. In former days the rival parties would doubtless have fought for it with their bands of armed retainers; but in more peaceful modern times it is safer, though not less expensive, to retain a small army of lawyers. The case has probably been locally investigated by a deputy collector, re-investigated and decided by a district collector, whose decision has been disputed before the commissioner, and now the final appeal lies to the Board of Revenue. This is merely a sample of the kind of cases which sometimes come before the members of the Board. In less important cases, or in cases between less wealthy and potent litigants, the services of counsel are almost invariably engaged, and several of the native pleaders who devote themselves to practise before the Board are almost unrivalled in their knowledge of all the details of revenue law, and also in the clearness and precision with which they state the facts and the points of their case. The appellate duties of the Board are much more important than is generally known or understood, and as in very many cases each member sits singly his labour is ordinarily quite as severe as that of any two judges of the High Court when sitting together as a bench.

The greater part of the Board's work is carried on by correspondence, partly with commissioners and partly with Government. The new letters are served up daily to each member in boxes, with all the important papers connected with each question. Lucid notes and suggestions are put up by the secretary subordinate to the member, so that the order to be issued can usually be passed with comparatively little difficulty, especially if the secretary is a man of practical experience and sound ability. There is, therefore, a smooth as well as a rough side to a seat in the Board. The member can, if he pleases, dispose of much of his correspondence in the quiet solitude of his own house. He is practically master of his own hours, and of his time for going to office and for leaving it. Sometimes a member spends the whole day at his office, and an instance has been known where a very zealous member actually took up his abode at the Board, so as to work uninterruptedly on some difficult subject on which he was engaged. On the other hand there have been members who only visited their office fitfully and carried on the greater part of their work at home. The members of the Board are also at liberty to make tours of inspection into the interior, and, in fact, they are authorised and encouraged by Government to make such tours, and occasionally they are expressly deputed by Government to visit a particular district to inquire and report upon some difficult question. So upon the whole the members of the Board lead a pleasant and well-employed life individually, although they often enjoy collectively the abuse and enmity of those who are under their authority; and, on the other hand, the Government usually takes advantage of the Board's intervention to give them the discredit of anything that does not turn out satisfactorily, and to appropriate to itself the credit of anything that has been done well. So that the Board still continues to fulfil its old mission as a convenient screen.

The public generally may be said to mistrust the Board, partly from its now suspected title, and partly because it has no proper appreciation of those very ponderous publications which are known as the Board's annual reports. The Board prepares and submits to Government an annual report on each principal subject that comes under its control. There is the annual report on the Land Revenue. There are annual reports on the Excise Department, on the Customs Department, on Salt, on Opium, on License-Tax, on Stamps, on Stationery, on the Shipping Office, and whatever other miscellaneous subject is susceptible of an annual report. Parliamentary Blue Books are light and cheerful reading in comparison with most of the Board's reports, but fortunately they find very few readers. Nevertheless annual reports may be said to represent the circulation of the blood in the whole official community. Every official throughout the country contributes his quota to them. The Board's reports may be compared to Aaron's rod, as they swallow up the reports of all their subordinates, and reproduce them for the edification of Government. For weeks, and even for months, some unfortunate clerks in the Board's office are toiling in the preparation of the rough drafts and the figured statements which form the basis of the Board's reports. The drafting clerk has the report of the previous year as his immediate model, and his chief duty is to incorporate in his draft the principal new facts and opinions which he can glean from the new reports of the officers subordinate to the Board. From time to time the clerk consults the secretary as the work progresses, and the day comes at last when the secretary takes the draft into his own hands, and polishes it up into a presentable shape. He then sends it off to the printer for a broad-margined proof, and in this shape it at last comes before the member of the Board, who has to read and revise it, and put in a few patches of adornment—or technical bunkum. When the report is thus complete, it is submitted to Government. When it has reached Government it is carefully analyzed by a secretariat clerk, who prepares the draft of a resolution on it. The Government secretary next dresses up the resolution and adds a few pungent remarks, and submits it for the approval of the Lieutenant-Governor. The Lieutenant-Governor is expected to read the resolution which issues under his authority, and it is to be hoped that he always does so. The Government resolution is then communicated to the Board, and the Board pass it on with a copy of their report to their subordinates, many of whom are anxiously looking out for it in the hope of official praise, and in dread of some inconvenient censure. And thus the report on each subject circulates throughout the whole framework of the official body; and subsides to rest until the coming of another year sets it again in motion. Each annual report may well bear the same motto, "*Adscribar numero, reddarque tenebris.*"

We have very nearly exhausted the catalogue of the various official duties to which a civilian may be required to devote himself in the course of his career. There are a few miscellaneous appointments connected with the post-office and the sea-customs, and opium and survey and registration, and there are the much-prized but very laborious offices which the secretaries of Government fill. But we will not weary our readers with further details. The Civil Service, as a body, are a hard-working and not over-paid set of men, considering the heavy responsibilities which are imposed upon them, and the great power which they have to exercise. There are very few men, save a few prudent bachelors, who are able to save anything like a competence from their incomes. A man with a wife and rising family soon finds his means consumed by the expenses of two establishments, one in India and another in England, and perhaps a third in the hills. There is no lack of youthful candidates who are induced to enter the service by the prospect of early independence and a secured income, which tempts some of them into early matrimony. But now that competition has introduced into the service so many men of a very high average ability, it may safely be said that almost all of them would have done as well for themselves in any of the liberal professions in England, if they could have afforded to wait at home till their opportunity came. It has been said that in some social points the men of the new school are not equal to those of the old school, but we doubt if this is susceptible of proof. There may be this difference between them. The hard-bargains of the old *régime* were chiefly their own enemies; the hard-bargains of the new *régime* sometimes manage to make themselves enemies by their own conceit and indocility. But we have every reason to believe and hope that the new race of men have already been found to be no unworthy successors to the traditions of the old service, and that they are a body of men in whose character and services the English nation may place full confidence.

CHAPTER VI.

NATIVE LIFE IN INDIA.

THERE are some people who seem to think that in writing about social life in India, the first place should be given to a consideration of the natives of the land. But we say it with sorrow, though without shame, that we can only add our testimony to that of many of the best friends of India, that the more an Englishman sees of India, the less competent he feels to write about the natives of the country. They are a good and loveable people, towards whom our hearts go forth only too readily, but we never seem to come to a true and thorough knowledge of them. The substance eludes our grasp, and we find ourselves contemplating an imaginary shadow. Possibly the day may come when some traveller like Miss Bird, who has given us such graphic accounts of the people of Japan and the Sandwich islands, may find her way to Bengal, and succeed in penetrating the veil of mystery. But up to the present time we know of no English writer who has been able thoroughly to master the whole subject. The natives themselves, from time to time, tell us something about themselves, and we find a very vivid picture of village life in Bengal in the admirable novel called "Gobind Samunt," which was written some years ago by the Rev. Lall Behari Dey. This, however, is a picture of the natives painted by one of themselves. What the English public want is a faithful picture of native life, drawn by an Englishman or a foreigner.

It is very natural to imagine that a member of the Civil Service has the most favourable opportunities of making himself acquainted with the natives. He certainly may have some advantages over non-official people, but, on the other hand, he is at many great disadvantages compared with non-official people. The official status puts him out of focus, if we may use the expression; he sees the natives under a false light, whilst they present themselves to his view with a fictitious colouring. Most of our readers have heard of Cicero and his writings and speeches. But it is not everyone who has read Cicero's treatise on the duties of a magistrate. We shall try to explain, on the authority of Cicero, how it comes to pass that in the exchange of intercourse between the Indian civilian and his native acquaintances, there is very much the same difficulty as there was between a Roman officer and the people of Asia Minor in days long past. It happened that when Cicero was one of the Consuls at

Rome, in the zenith of his power, he had a brother named Quintus, who was proprætor or governor of Asia Minor. The ordinary term of a proprætor's government seems to have been for two years, but Cicero managed to get an extension of service for his brother for a third year. In sending the good news to his brother, Cicero took the opportunity of writing him a lecture, partly to show his own superior knowledge of all sublunary things, and partly because it is tolerably clear that the brother required a lecture. A little good advice might do him good, and it could not do him any harm. He was evidently an irascible, overbearing man, but Cicero particularly desires it to be understood that his hands were pure, and that he took no bribes. Admitting this to be so, he seems to have stood very much in the position which the Indian civilian sometimes fills. He too is often suspected of being irascible and overbearing, and is, fortunately, not often accused of any want of honesty or high principle.

With regard to the people of Asia Minor, Cicero writes that the province is composed first of that kind of allies who, of all the human race, are the most humanised, and in the next place, of those Roman citizens who are either farmers of the public revenue or have become rich by trade. Yet, he observes, "even among these men serious disputes exist, many injustices are committed, and great contentions are the consequence." Here, then, we have a sort of parallel with the people of India. The natives themselves are proud of a civilisation which dates back to a period long anterior to our own. There are English merchants and planters and jute manufacturers settled in India, some of whom become rich, and are also, unhappily, not free from disputes between themselves and with the natives.

Cicero warns his brother to be careful that the inhabitants are not alarmed at his journeys, that they are not frightened by his approach; that there should be the utmost rejoicing, both public and private, wherever he goes; that every town should seem to receive him as its guardian, not as its tyrant. Do not these remarks call to mind the progress of great Indian officials with their large camps and retainers innumerable, who are only too apt to prey upon the people of the country through which they pass, unless the most vigilant supervision is maintained? Even the smallest civilian who goes out into camp in his district will find that unless he himself sees that everything is paid for, his servants and followers will endeavour to live at free quarters in the name of their master.

Cicero says to his brother: "Let all the province be sensible how dearly you prize the welfare, the children, the fame and the fortunes of all who are under your command. Let it be notorious that you will be equally the enemy of the man who gives a present as of him who receives it; for no one will give when it is clearly perceived that those who pretend to have the greatest interest with you are accustomed to obtain nothing from you. It is not that I would have you treat your dependants in a too severe and suspicious manner. If you have got any person who has been thoroughly admitted to your intimacy, consider how far you ought to trust him—not but that there may be many worthy men amongst the provincials, this it is lawful to hope but dangerous to determine; for every man's nature is concealed with many folds of disguise and covered with various veils. His nature, his brows, his eyes and his countenance are deceitful; and his speech is most commonly a lie. Where can you find one who will sincerely love you, a mere stranger to them, and not merely pretend to do so for his own advantage? It would seem to me strange, as these men seldom pay any regard to private men, while they invariably attach themselves to the prætors. If amongst such men you should find one (for the thing is not impossible) who loves you more than he does his own interests, enrol him as a friend; but if you do not perceive this, there is no class of acquaintance more to be avoided; because they know all the arts of getting money, they do nothing but for money, and they are indifferent about the opinion of any man with whom they are not to continue to live. For the Greeks in general are deceitful and treacherous, and trained up by perpetual subjection in the art of sycophancy. All of them should be liberally treated, and the best of them received into friendship; but too close intimacies with them are not very safe, for though they dare not oppose your wishes, yet they are jealous not only of our countrymen, but even of their own. Though they dare not fly in the face of a Roman magistrate, yet at the bottom they hate not only us but their own countrymen."

Those who have been invested with the official authority which a civilian exercises during his career in India can most easily tell how much there is in the warnings of Cicero which comes home to their feelings. Accustomed to receive every outward token of respect and affection, they are hardly willing to ask themselves the question why it was that such regard to themselves as public officers was paid by the men who seldom show much regard to any private men. Have they never felt, when circumstances caused them to be transferred from one district to another, how indifferent their former admirers soon became towards the man with whom they were no longer to continue to live?

From the very beginning of his career the civilian is put in a peculiar position as to his native surroundings. He has no difficulty in obtaining domestic servants. He will do well to understand that in India, as perhaps in other countries, although the master fancies that he is selecting a servant, it is in reality the servant who chooses his master. The master is a sort of speculation into which the servant enters, if it suits his convenience and is likely to pay. A young civilian is certain to have a good income and a respectable expenditure, out of which the servant may make a profit. The young civilian will also exercise official authority, and the servant speculates that he will make some pickings out of it. A civilian in high authority once remonstrated with his servant, who professed to complain of too much work, and asked him why, if he was dissatisfied, he did not take service with some rich Calcutta merchant whose whole day was spent at his office. "Sir," replied the man, "they have no visitors." Whenever a native gentleman comes to call at the house of a high official, the native servants always expect a fee. The visitor pays it, for the amount is not large, and he does not know what might happen if he did not pay. There are many petty slights, or really insults, which the servants could pass upon him with impunity if he did not render the accustomed tribute. And thus it comes to pass that a civilian has no difficulty in obtaining and keeping his native servants, provided that he treats them with reasonable kindness and due consideration for their shortcomings towards himself. The native servants who surround a young man at the beginning of his career sometimes have a considerable influence on his subsequent demeanour towards all other natives. It usually happens that a young man is delighted with some of his first native servants, whom he finds so intelligent and attentive and desirous of pleasing him. The servant rises to the occasion, and is not slow to attempt to help his master in matters which ought not to be a subject of communication between them. But the cause and effect are very natural. The master returns home weary from his office, and has no one to speak to but his servant. He casually mentions something that has happened in office during the day, or perhaps tries to ascertain from his servant if he has rightly understood some explanation given to him in the course of business. The servant is not slow to profit by such an opportunity. When his master has gone to bed the servant speeds off to the native town, and soon finds out the particular case to which his master must have alluded. He is thus in a position to make the parties interested in the case believe that he can influence his master on the subject, and the possession of such a power is, of course, equivalent to a mine of wealth. We can vouch for the truth of a story regarding the head-servant of an officer, who never exchanged a word with him on any official business. But the servant was sufficiently clever to make outsiders believe that he had great influence with his master, and the time came when he gracefully retired from his master's service, and went home to his native village to figure as a landed proprietor, with a herd of several hundred head of cattle! Well might Cicero warn the proprætor of Asia Minor against putting too much confidence in his own domestics, or in permitting them to abuse the show of his authority.

We next come to the civilian in his public office,

where by the necessity of the case he is surrounded and assisted by native subordinates of various ranks and degrees of authority. These native subordinates are to the English civilian in India somewhat in the same position as the permanent clerks in an English Government Office to the temporary ministerial secretary. The civilian changes office only too frequently. He is transferred from one district to another. To-day he is an assistant at Dacca, to-morrow he is joint-magistrate at Patna. The next day he is collector at Calcutta. But wherever he goes he finds himself introduced to a set of grave, white-robed native officers, from whom he must try to learn much of what has gone before, and through whom he must conduct the business of the office in which he presides. Many of these men have no want of ability or experience. They have received some education, and now-a-days are more or less conversant with the English language. But their salaries are small, and though they are much higher than the salaries of former times, they are still insufficient to meet the ever-increasing wants of modern civilisation and expenditure. Each of these men will do his best to ingratiate himself with his civilian superior. They try to help him in all his difficulties, and are ready to devote themselves to the execution of all his orders. Hence it very naturally follows that their superior takes a lively interest in them and welcomes their aid; but it also very frequently follows that some of them succeed in gaining a greater amount of favour than their fellows. Not unfrequently one man becomes his master's special favourite and adviser. The sahib learns to see everything through his favourite's spectacles, and to be guided, however unconsciously, by his suggestions and promptings. The result is inevitable. Those who have failed to gain favour combine and intrigue against the favourite—but their machinations fail. There is however, a Nemesis in store. The civilian is transferred, and another officer takes his place. The old favourite makes a struggle to maintain his position and authority with the new man, but probably in vain. The mere fact that he was a favourite with Mr. A—— is sufficient to discredit him with Mr. B——; and it sometimes, on the other hand, happens that the native officer whose influence with Mr. A—— was supreme finds himself utterly indisposed and unwilling to render the same allegiance to Mr. B——, however much Mr. B—— may have been inclined to appreciate him.

The next grade of native officials with whom the young civilian comes in contact are the officers styled deputy collectors and deputy magistrates, who exercise a very large amount of anthority, and constitute the chief administrative staff of each district. These gentlemen are usually men of large practical experience, and if the young civilian has the good fortune to make a friendly acquaintance with any of them he will find them most valuable and useful friends and allies. He can consult them with confidence in any matters that are new to him, and they will gladly help him in his official anxieties. But whilst the native deputy demeans himself with due consideration and respect to all those who are or may be in authority over him, there are some of them who do not always lay their hearts open to the advances of a young civilian. The old-fashioned deputy who had risen from the ranks of practical experience, and had never troubled himself with the study of the English language, was usually a trustworthy friend. But in recent times the graduates of the Calcutta university, with their English accomplishments and classical diplomas, have filled the office of deputies, and they are not unusually of opinion that they could do all the official work of the country much better than the young Englishmen who are sent out to manage the districts and practically rule the country. It is much to be deplored, but it is unfortunately the fact that an education in the English-teaching schools and colleges does not ordinarily generate a sense of affection for the English Government or its representatives. The result is not unnatural. They have eaten of the fruit of the tree of knowledge, and find that they are naked. They see their English rulers in the enjoyment of the best things which they naturally think should have fallen to their lot, and they are not disposed to be content with the good things which they have obtained under the English Government. They see that their English rulers are always ready to improve their position, and (not to put too fine a point on it) to increase their pay. So they constantly agitate for more pay and more power, and renewed concessions have only the effect of producing increased demands. Whether any concessions will satisfy them is quite another question. When the subordinate native judges, some years ago, had their pay increased from £600 to £1,200 a year, one of them called on a civilian judge, who proceeded to congratulate him on his good fortune. "I am quite disgusted, Sir!" replied the native gentleman. "I wanted to be appointed to the Patna district, and the Lieutenant-Governor has appointed me to Hooghly." He did not pretend to care for the increased pay which he had obtained, but he still wanted something more. With regard to almost any officer in this position of well-paid independence, it might safely be predicated that if there had been no English Government to provide him with employment his paternal acres would have seldom yielded him an income of £50 a year, and possibly, as the retainer of some great man, he might have earned another £20 a year by some sort of service. But under no form of oriental native government would he have dreamt of a salary of £1,200 a year to be followed by a retiring pension of £600 a year. Very few people are aware of the very great strides by which the salaries of native officers have increased. We could name four able men, members of a middle class but talented native family, who before 1850 were collectively drawing pay which gave them £400 a year, and they were not discontented. In 1870, these same four men had so floated upwards with the stream that their united income was not less than £4,000 a year, and still they were hoping for more.

We began this paper by protesting against the incompetence of an Englishman to give a satisfactory account of the natives of India. But we will now give a special reason for this. The women of the country are a sealed book to the stranger. He has no opportunity of seeing them or speaking to them, and he can learn very little about them. Let anyone imagine the case of a native Indian gentleman coming to England, or France, or America, and having his eyes closed to the whole of the female population. In India, as long as a woman has any youth and beauty she is kept in strict seclusion from the public gaze. In large towns in certain quarters a few painted Jezebels may be seen looking down from their upper stories, but otherwise an European visitor might believe that youth and beauty did not exist in the land. And not only does the eye never behold the best portion of the female sex, but a rigid etiquette must be observed in conversation with a native gentleman in even alluding to the female members of his household. But it is not to be supposed that women in India do not exercise a considerable influence upon the men. They are doubtless good mothers, good wives, and affectionate sisters. They have their strong religious feelings, and are seldom negligent of the duties connected with the domestic worship of their household gods. But to the foreigners they are practically unknown. One might as well attempt to give an account of the terrestrial system, recognising the power of the sun, but utterly ignoring all the more genial influences of the moon. Perhaps the time may come when the women of India may assert themselves more publicly, and insist on the enjoyment of those privileges which their European sisters have as their birthright; but until that time comes, how can any Englishman venture to write about the real people of India? A civilian has no more true knowledge of the female portion of the native population than a native has of the members of the English peerage. Even in his court, as a magistrate, women are seldom brought forward, either as criminals or witnesses, though occasionally some sort of she-wolf is arraigned for having murdered some unfortunate child for the sake of its ornaments. Or it may be that some quarrel about a woman has led to a murderous dispute, and perhaps a muffled bundle of clothes said to contain a female is produced as a witness in the case before him. But it is exceedingly difficult even to understand the language as spoken by a woman, and he would certainly be a bold person who would venture to generalise on the national female character from such specimens as he may casually see from time to time in court.

Still we are unwilling not to record a grateful reminiscence of the many kindnesses which we have received at the hands of many influential and wealthy native friends. How could our official duties have been performed with any amount of satisfaction or success, without the able and intelligent assistance so freely and zealously rendered by those over whom we were set in authority? And how can we forbear from acknowledging the long and unwearying faithful services of successive generations of native servants, who so often anticipated our wishes and carried out our orders to the best of their ability!

It is the privilege of every civilian officer to have the opportunity of becoming acquainted with the principal native gentlemen of the district in which he is employed. Soon after his arrival at a new station they come to call on him; whilst those who live within a convenient distance, and are inclined to be sociable, repeat their visits at intervals. There are, unfortunately, some native gentlemen who seem to think it unnecessary or undesirable to make such calls; and as the ways and habits of different civilians differ considerably, there are some officers who do not encourage such visits, so that their successors have some difficulty in making it known that they will gladly receive visitors. It is unnecessary to analyse too minutely the particular object which each visitor has in calling; but it is much better for a civilian to run the risk of any abuse of the opportunity by his visitor, than to shut his door upon a mere suspicion. Most native gentlemen are far too honourable to attempt any allusion in the course of their visit to any subject which it would be unbecoming to mention; and if any such attempt were made, it is easily in the power of the officer receiving the visit to put the subject aside with due regard to his own dignity. But the benefit, and pleasure, and information which are to be derived from such visits far outweigh any inconvenience or annoyance that may possibly arise from them. It is true that a portly native gentleman, whilst uttering the usual formal compliments of introduction, does not always remember to suppress those ebullitions which are considered amongst his own people to be indicative of his having enjoyed his breakfast; it is true that the language of polite flattery is sometimes rather over-strained; but when the first effervescence of such frothy nothings has subsided, the time will come when the visitor will work down to his natural powers of conversation, according to the capacity which he possesses. It is to be observed that two native gentlemen calling at the same time prefer to be received separately, unless, of course, they have some common object in calling; but, on the other hand, an officer in a high position will often find his advantage in having his visitors admitted simultaneously, especially if he has one day of the week particularly set apart for the reception of his native visitors.

But it may be said that these kind of visits do not amount to social intercouse. Certainly not. Nor, on the other hand, do we admit that there is any social intercourse, in the true meaning of the word, where the official goes to a party at the house of a wealthy native gentleman, to some special entertainment such as a nautch or fireworks in honour of a wedding or any other domestic occurrence. It will be admitted that two of the main elements of social intercourse accordin to English ideas consist (1) in dining together, (2) in the interchange of ladies' society. But the native getleman will seldom come to dine with the English gentleman; and although an English lady has no objection to receive the visit of a native gentleman, or to go to his entertainments, there seems to be little prospect at present of seeing a native lady come forth to welcome the English visitors at her husband's house. Behind the mere external difficulties there come all the complications of caste and religious observance, and also of dress, of which the etiquette is almost unfathomable. The natives themselves are not in accord with one another on many points which come into prominence in their contact with English society; and although many parties are now given in the capital of Calcutta and in other large towns by high officials on the one hand, and by native gentlemen on the other hand, where people of both races meet for one or two hours, we fear that on such occasions there is very little real mutual enjoyment, and that the hosts are usually very glad when the last of the guests has departed.

Several wealthy native noblemen and gentlemen in the interior keep a neatly-furnished bungalow or house, in which they can entertain their English friends who visit them on their estates for the sake of hunting and shooting. In the Burdwan district the late Maharajah used in former years to entertain parties of his English friends at the Dilkoosha and Kishensaugor garden-houses, especially at the time of the Burdwan Races. We could name several other similar places, but we must give the preference to the recollection of the happy days spent in the country house of our good old friend Rajah Kalinaraian Roy of Dacca. He had built a suite of apartments contiguous to his own old native palace, and it was his pleasure to invite his English friends from Dacca to come out and stay with him, to shoot tigers and hunt wild hogs. His property was very extensive, and contained a great portion of the Madhupore jungle, which runs more than fifty miles to the north of Dacca, with an average breadth of about ten miles. The ground is undulating and slightly hilly in parts, and is well intersected with streams of fresh water, so that it afforded a good harbour for all sorts of game, tigers, leopards, bears, buffaloes, sambur and spotted and hog deer, and a few wild boars, with a fair sprinkling of hares and partridges and jungle-fowl, and occasionally a woodcock. An easy drive of about twenty miles from Dacca brought the visitors to the Rajah's palace, where the Rajah was sure to be ready to greet them on their arrival. He was a fine-looking man, with pleasant features and a strong vigorous figure. When he came out to join the shooting-party on his elephant he used to be stripped to the waist, and his shoulders and chest were covered with thick grey hairs, which were suggestive of the *στηθεσσιν λασιοισι* of Homer. A little fillet of white muslin bound round his temples protected his head from the sun; but of course his servant behind him in the howdah always carried an umbrella. He had a good battery of guns and rifles, and was a very good shot. It was almost always a sure sign that there was a tiger to be got when the Rajah came out with the party. The visitors were always ready to go out at any time to shoot whatever turned up, as they had come out for perhaps only a few days' holiday and must take their chance. One great advantage of the shooting at the Rajah's was that we usually went after a tiger on receiving information of "a kill." An excited peasant would come rushing in with the news that his cow had just been killed, and imploring the Rajah to go out to take revenge. It was a pleasure to see the Rajah's face when he felt sure that the information was true, and from his knowledge of the country he also was certain that the tiger was watching the carcase from a patch of cover which could be conveniently beaten by the elephants. By approaching the cover judiciously, and with due regard to the wind, we were almost certain to find a tiger, and it was our fault if it was not killed.

The Rajah was a large landholder, and the visitors at his house had a most favourable opportunity of seeing how he managed his property and conducted his affairs with his tenants and his neighbours. The people flocked in daily in considerable numbers to attend the Rajah's office, and if they had leisure they would come and have a good stare at the English visitors. The principal part of the office-work was carried on by the Rajah's native ministerial officers of various grades and titles; but he almost invariably took his seat in office for an hour or two, and had no objection to our going to hear what passed between him and his people, for he was always courteous and considerate to them, and their complaints and grievances were not often directed against him, but were chiefly the result of petty disputes among themselves about caste and other such matters of which the Rajah was a highly competent judge. He would occasionally order a fine to be paid, or compensation to be levied from the delinquent party, and disregard to such an order was seldom exhibited. It sometimes happened that our visits to the Rajah's palace were paid on the native holidays and festivals; and on these occasions the whole country-side used to flock to the entertainments given at the Rajah's expense. It is hardly necessary to say that he distributed charitable gifts in food and money day by day to a considerable number of religious mendicants and professional beggars; but on the great holidays or festivals the expenditure of gratuitous food was something enormous, and due respect was shown to the visitors according to their various ranks and grades in native society. Music and song and dancing would last long past midnight, and few of the guests were allowed to go away empty-handed. It would be difficult to imagine a more genial and healthy state of relations than that which existed generally on the Rajah's estates between him and his people. Doubtless many of them were poor and ignorant, but the mild despotism with which the Rajah ruled them required very little tempering from the interference of English law or officials.

With regard to his English visitors, the Rajah showed the kindest hospitality. He did not object if they took out their own provisions and wines, and their own cook, for the better preservation of their own health. But the Rajah always had supplies of food provided for his visitors, and his wines were undoubtedly the most costly that could be purchased by him from the Armenian shops in Dacca. The Rajah would usually look in to see his visitors when breakfast was nearly over, and preparations were beginning for the day's sport. But his great delight was to come in at dessert when the visitors had done their dinner, and he would not object to smoke a quiet cigar with them. He was full of fun, and liked his little jokes and puns, especially if any visitor had any knowledge of the Persian language to enable the Rajah to show his proficiency in that tongue. For the Rajah did not know English, his education having been completed in the olden time, when Persian was the Court and fashionable language. He was full of anecdotes connected with shooting, and the various adventures with tigers in which he had shared with the best sportsmen from Dacca for a long course of years. He was a capital mimic, and it was easy to recognise his imitation of some of the old sportsmen in their moments of excitement. He used to have his little son and daughter brought into the room in their smartest native dresses. The son has now grown up, and is a worthy and liberal successor to his father. The daughter came very quickly to the marriageable age, and after she was married it was no longer permissible for her to come down and talk to strange gentlemen. But she used to take opportunities of seeing the visitors, she herself being unseen; and, as a fact, the visitors were almost always paraded quietly so that they might be seen by all the ladies of the Rajah's household. He had two wives, of whom the eldest was childless, the second wife being the mother of his two children. To those with whom he was best acquainted he was in the habit of discoursing about his domestic affairs, and, if imperious native custom had not forbidden it, we believe that he would have been very willing to have introduced them to his wives. When English ladies were of the party, they were always taken into the inner apartments to make the acquaintance of the ladies. Perhaps one of the most curious illustrations of the incongruity of native and English feeling occurred during one of our visits. The Rajah's daughter had been married to a Kulin Brahmin of the highest caste, who lived with her at the Rajah's palace. But as he was a man of specially high caste, it was his privilege to be married to any number of wives whose parents could pay for their espousal to him. And so we became accidentally witnesses of the occasion on which the young husband set forth with a grand marriage procession from his own first wife's house, in order to be married to another young lady of high family. It is an Hindoo institution, and it was not in the Rajah's power to resist it for his own daughter's sake. But to the English visitors, especially to the ladies who were present, the whole proceeding seemed very uncomfortable, and the more so as we were fully aware that the Rajah and his daughter were, in their inmost hearts, most averse to what was taking place.

As we have ventured to write of our old Hindoo friend, Rajah Kalinaraian Roy, we feel bound to speak in no less grateful terms of the chief Mahomedan zemindars in Dacca, the Nawab Khajeh Abdul Gunnee, and his son, the Nawab Khajeh Ahsanoollah. They too had a shooting-box at a convenient distance from Dacca, to which they would invite their English friends, and they kept a stud of about twenty elephants, some of which were of the finest and staunchest of their kind. They were most liberal and good-natured in lending their elephants to those whom they could trust, though there were always plenty of elephants at Dacca, as it is the head-quarters of the Government elephant depôt. Many years after I had left Dacca, they sent a couple of elephants to meet a friend of mine nearly a hundred miles from Dacca, when he wanted them with the Calcutta Tent Club. In every public and private work of utility and charity both father and son were equally munificent. They sent their handsome contributions to the subscriptions raised for various charitable purposes in England. They were always amongst the first to give whatever was needed for the improvement of the town and district of Dacca, and for the good of its inhabitants. To the poor and needy they never turned a deaf ear, and whenever an opportunity presented itself they were always ready with their handsome entertainments in honour of the Lieutenant-Governors or any other great people who visited Dacca. We wish them long life and prosperity. But we must reluctantly put an end to the record of those many pleasant days which we spent in Dacca, nearly twenty years ago, with this imperfect acknowledgment of how much was due to the kindness of our Hindoo and Mahomedan friends there.